LIFE'S JOURNEY
THROUGH THE EYES
OF
A POET

by John Weldon Evans

DEDICATED
To
GRACEY.INGLETON

One of her many gifts was sponsoring
wonderful group trips abroad.
Without her, I would never have been to
Africa twice, Australia, China, and
the Mediterranean

Introduction

Life's Journey Through the Eyes of a Poet is a book of poems organized under the sub-titles:

I.   Freedom, Equality, Humanity (14 poems)
II.   Life's Four Seasons (16 poems)
III.   Love (19 poems)
IV.   Travelling Abroad (15 poems)
V.   Reflections (28 poems)
VI.   Remembrances (26 poems)
VII.   Come Walk With Me Down Memory Lane and Other Poems
        (4 poems)

Section I: In the poems Freedom, Equality, Humanity, the author writes about the massive migration of black people from the south in the early nineteen hundreds to escape from white oppression, intimidation, racial injustice, and poverty. He chooses to focus on the migration particularly to the region of Harlem (where he taught for 40 years) and writes about its birth, evolution and rise to become a mecca of black culture, intelligence, empowerment, religion, music and art, only to decline in the later 20th century. Other poems in this section deal with black people's struggles against racism and the hypocrisy of equal justice for all that black people never seem to enjoy. In the poem, Souls of Black People are a River, he writes of the millions of black souls victimized through centuries of slavery whose blood form a river of human suffering and carnage. He calls out hatred and fear in the poem Prison Walls... as a senseless barrier buried deep within the human heart imprisoning all of us, black and white.

Hate has no conscience, guilt, nor logic, consumes itself with endless thirst, builds nothing, saves nothing, heals nothing and destroys both the hater and the hated. As in the poem, The Enigma, love falls on deaf ears; we should all dread that God should punish us for our hatred. Better to be a dreamer than a hater. As in, I Am A Dreamer, great men have always been dreamers.

Section II: In Life's Four Seasons the author views life through the lens of Nature, with man's evolution similar to that of nature. Spring, equivalent to our birth and childhood; Summer, to our youth; autumn, to our adulthood; and winter, to our old age. May be, as in the poem, Winter Sonnet, spring will return (in another realm perhaps) after the winter of old age, as the poem hopes for.)

Section III: Love - The greatest force in nature and perhaps the universe. The author believes that in all of nature, love is the most magnificent, most attractive force both for man and for all the creatures who multiply. The only difference with humans is that we are more complicated. We think too much, and dream too much, and shed too much tears, sometimes. There are 19 poems in this section, and the author's favorite is: I Had Thought To Love Was Best. Eternal Love is also a favorite, though it involves martyrdom.

Section IV: Travelling Abroad to the countries of Ghana, Egypt, China, Australia, New Zealand, and Fiji, the first observation the writer made was that although all people are different, yet they are the same. God's creatures may wear different clothes and speak different languages, but they all have the same hopes, dreams, needs, and mortality. Where they are different, they are very fascinating. In the Blue Mountains of Australia they have strange legends about the land and about natural phenomena, as in the story about the 'three sisters' in the Blue Mountains poem. In China, the Great Wall of Beijing, the Jade Factory, the Silk Factory, for each one of them the author has written a poem. For Ghana he writes a poem about the haunted slave dungeons where his ancestors were chained and horribly treated before being loaded onto slave ships. The monuments of Egypt, the pyramids, the sphynx, The valley of the Dead, all have their poems in this section also.

Section V: Reflections. Here the writer is more spiritual and philosophical. Life is a paradox and we lose perfection when we lose our childhood. As we continue living, simultaneously our bodies are dying. We are all our brother's keeper (Implied in the poem I Never Walk Alone). Life is the greatest journey, the greatest battle, the greatest road to victory (as in The Greatest Journey). Life is fleeting, waste not a moment, you can never buy back time. These sayings are implied in the poems: The Old Lady; If I Could Save Up Time; and The Old Man With a Cane.

We are all spiritual entities occupying a physical body, and our spirit will someday fly away just like an eagle (as implied in the poem, Something About an Eagle Soaring). The earth is dying, and it will, if we do not save it. (See the poem Save the Earth From Dying.)

The writer believes there is only one road that leads to a worthwhile end --
the road to God (as in the lesson taught in The Man, The River, The Bridge,
and The Moon), and the perfection in man that God seeks is an humble and
a contrite heart, (as in the poem, The Masterpiece.) Old Age at least deserves
a purple heart for all it has gone through in the struggle of life (as in Youth
Vs Old Age). The author believes that no one wishes to be the last human
being on earth (as in Who Will Be The Last to Cry.)

Section VI: Remembrances is a collection of (26) poems dedicated to family
and close friends who were a part of the writer's early development and adult
years. Without them his journey could not have taken place.

Section VII: In the final section, Come Walk With Me Down Memory Lane
and Other Poems, the poet takes the reader along with him on a casual stroll
back in time to his birthplace, La Boca, C.Z., which he calls, Memory Town,
and the streets and sidewalks, Memory Lane. A few other poems are added
such as: "Land Where My Father Labored and Died" which is about the
Silver People's resting place in Corozal, P.C.Z.where his parents are buried;
"The Old Timer," which is about an old Panama Canal construction worker
who lived in Washapali, Panama and whom the writer visited just before his
passing (when the U.S. invaded Panama); and finally, the closing poem:
"Wayfarer, Wayfarer, Where is Your Home," a fitting ending since the
writer's home, La Boca, C.Z., was demolished and vanished from the earth.

TABLE OF CONTENTS

III. Love

IV. Travelling In Distant Lands

V. Reflections

VI. Poems Of Rememberances

I.   FREEDOM, EQUALITY, AND HUMANITY

Harlem

Some places start out with odds against them.
If you ask me, such a place was Harlem.
I don't mean the Harlem of today,
nor the Harlem the builders planned their way.
But I speak of the Harlem that once came to be
out of necessity or accidentally,
or maybe it was destiny.
In any case, it is now history.

Long before there were settlers in these lands,
there were Indian tribes like the Manhattans.
Then came the pilgrims, and we know their history
and the fate of the Indians, but that's another story.
Europeans settled here, suffice it to say,
and gave it its name that it bears to this day.

The Harlem we knew was once a scene,
in the Revolutionary War that was fought between
the British and George Washington's colonial army.
It was called the Battle of Haarlem, was fought fiercely,
on the west side near one hundred twenty-fifth Street,
and it was a surprising British defeat.
The British had headquartered in lower Manhattan,
and Washington had fortified the area of Haarlem.
His headquarters was in the Jumel Mansion
overlooking the Polo Grounds (formerly Giant Stadium).
In seventeen 'seventy-six' the skirmish
took place when Washington routed the British
even though outnumbered more than two-to-one,
and drove them back to one Hundred Sixth Street, stunned;
but the British returned and burned Haarlem to the ground.
The war lasted eight years, and, of course, the rebels won.
After the war, there were many estates around
in the regions that were spread out with lots of farmlands
settled by immigrants from the Netherlands,
and owned by wealthy families like the Bensons,
Van Keulens, Randalls, Roosevelts, and Hamiltons.

Building up the area of Harlem, though,
took some time and at first was very slow,
for the region remained largely rural, and there was no
transportation except steamboats on the East River
and stagecoaches through Central Park and in winter
the East River froze up. After eighteen thirty-one
Harlem did not remain sparse for too long.
The N.Y.- Harlem R.R. (Metro North)
was built, which planted a seed for growth,
linking the region of Harlem with the city
and with the north up to Westchester County.
First, a couple of wealthy land speculators
(Charles Henry Hall was one, and soon others..)
invested in her potentialities,
building infrastructure, streets, facilities,
gas lines, sewer lines for urban living.
Some statesmen and businessmen joined in
and they made Harlem their country retreat.
Soon, it was growing into a village, albeit
not for the rich alone but the poor as well
who could find low-rent dwellings and employment.
By eighteen seventy, with the advent
of the demise of estates that were broken up
and auctioned off when farmlands dried up,
squatters moved in, and the area was depressed,
in real estate values. This, coupled with the stress,
of the depression of eighteen seventy-three,
gave the City of New York the opportunity
to step in and annex the region known as Harlem,
all the way to one fifty-fifth Street, implementing,
a program called Urban Renewal Planning.

They built the Westside and Eastside "els,"
and started the Lexington and IRT lines as well.
Developers rushed in and, after eighteen eighty,
constructed new buildings in the Harlem community.
Many row houses and multiple-family apartment
dwellings were built. With rapid development,
builders expected white people from downtown,
and elsewhere to rush to their paradise uptown
with fine townhouses and apartments, an outright
entrepreneur's dream, which they had in sight,
society of wealth, polo, high taste, and fashion,
with even an opera house to fulfill their passion.

Then a real estate crash in the nineties spelled doom
to their hasty and extravagant building boom,
and the whites did not rush to fill their dream town,
so they were left with a glut of housing uptown.

With a steep drop in value during this phase,
it became a buyer's market that attracted waves
of immigrant European Jews and Italians
to east Harlem, flooding it by the thousands,
creating a Jewish neighborhood and a little Italy
that would be replaced by Puerto Ricans eventually,
along the east side south of One-sixteenth Street.
But this didn't fill the glut in Harlem, so to meet
their desperate plight, landlords next turned to
a black realtor, a black entrepreneur who
could solve their problem, and that was when
Phillip A. Payton stepped in, and he then,
with his Afro-American Realty Company,
had no trouble filling up the Harlem community
once landlords agreed to let blacks move in…
and it's funny how greed changed the color of skin.

The first wave of blacks came from mid-town and downtown
where they faced anti-black riots in those parts of town,
especially neighborhoods like Tenderloin
(a red light district that was near mid-town),
San Juan Hill (where Lincoln Center is today),
Minetta Lane (called Negroes Causeway
and Little Africa by whites), located in
Greenwich Village (where ex-slaves were living
and were, unfortunately, too often prone
to be victims and to be preyed upon);
also, there was Hell's Kitchen, a community
of Irish immigrants where blacks had no identity.

Up in Harlem, as blacks moved in, whites moved out,
which soon became a familiar pattern throughout;
and that's how Harlem opened for blacks to come,
including blacks from the Caribbean, who were welcome.
Of course, they were cheated and charged higher rents
than the rates that were charged the white tenants;
and landlords squeezed blacks into smaller apartments,
collecting high rents without making improvements.
Anyway, the time was ripe for blacks to come
to Harlem -- it was the dawn of the Great Migration.

Before eighteen sixty-five, there were less
than eight per cent Afro-Americans at best
who were living in northern cities alone;
but by the nineteen fifties, the figure had grown
to seven million who came primarily from the South
where the burning desire and will was to get out
because of poverty, oppression, wages too low,
and they couldn't vote and were stifled by Jim Crow.

They came north by bus, by car, and by train;
some even came by boat, and then again,
by any and every possible means, they came.
Whatever the means, the result was the same.
They came from the cotton fields of Mississippi,
from the coal mines and steel mills of Tennessee,
from the farms and coal mines of Alabama,
the docks of Virginia, Georgia, Texas, Louisiana.
It was the Great Northern Migration
and it changed the makeup of this nation.

The human spirit and the will to survive
will drive men to seek a better way to live.
How would it be where they were going?
Who would go first, going without knowing?
How would they live? What would it cost?
It did not matter whatever the cost.
It did not matter whatever they lacked,
though Hell should bar the way, there was no turning back.
No more lynching and torture and hopelessness.
Only one choice: it was freedom and nothing less.

So, the Afro-American exodus went forth
like an irresistible force from the South,
As one Alabamian, "Cow Cow" Davenport, wrote,
in his song "Jim Crow Blues," from which I quote:
"Tired o' being Jim Crowed, gonna leave Jim Crow town.
Doggone, my black soul, I'm sweet Chicago bound.
Yes, sir, I'm leaving here from this ole Jim Crow town.
I'm goin up north, where they think money grows on trees;
an' I don't give a doggone if ma black soul should freeze,
I'm goin' where I don't need no B.V.D.'s."

Prospects up north were greater in every way.
There were plenty of jobs and better pay
due to expansion of many large industries
and the shortage of workers in the big cities.
Schools were better where their children could go,
so they said, "Farewell, we're gone, Jim Crow!"
Heading north, they crossed over the Mason-Dixon,
going northeast, Midwest, west, and so on.
They poured into northern towns like Chicago,
New York City, Cleveland, Detroit, San Francisco
and numerous others I need not mention.
All told, during the Great Black Migration
the two most popular places were South Chicago
and Central Harlem. Harlem, though,
became the densest four square miles
anywhere in this country population-wise,
with two hundred fifteen thousand per square mile
living in her borders on Manhattan Isle,
from the East River to the Hudson River in width,
its length, ninety-sixth Street to one hundred fifty-fifth.
Of course, overcrowding brought challenges,
that were no different than in growing cities,
issues that politics and governments should rectify,
with all of the tensions that task would imply.

Harlem, a place destined for greatness,
destined for sadness, brightness, and darkness,
hope and despair was a beacon, nonetheless,
for the hearts and souls of black Americans.
They came there in the hundreds of thousands
seeking freedom from blatant oppression,
from poverty and endless intimidation,
yearning for, seeking for opportunities
to live and control their own destinies.

Harlem, a place that was chosen for a reason:
so the souls of black people could have a season,
so their aspirations once stifled, enchained,
could have a place where unconstrained,
they would voice their passions and their pain,
express their intellect, talents ordained,
through art, essays, music, poetry, and song,
religion, sports (from boxing to the gridiron);

Harlem, where the greatest black minds and talent
gathered and formed an enlightened new movement,
a new line of thought, new standard of beauty,
new kind of racial love, respect, and identity,
creating their own art from their heritage and history,
shedding forever old images of inferiority,
was a Mecca of a new consciousness, a new voice
in music, art, politics, and every field of choice.

Harlem, home of the New Negro Movement,
the Harlem Renaissance that was nascent
in nineteen seventeen, with its first publication,
"The Voice," founded by Hubert Harrison,
was energized with a new black radicalism
that demanded equality and an end to racism,
and was the driving force that gave exposure
to great writers of Afro-American literature:
Langston Hughes, Claude McKay, Zora Neale Hurston,
Jean Toomer, Jessie Fauset, Countee Cullen,
to intellectuals such as Alain Locke, who
was a thinker and editor of the "New Negro,"

Marcus Garvey, the greatest black unity champion
who founded a universal black association,
W. E. B. DuBois, distinguished historian,
co-founder of the N.A.A.C.P. and
brilliant scholar whose goal intellectually
was the destruction of the policy of white supremacy.

Harlem, a Godsend to black gifts and aspirations,
to black dreams yearning, seeking to find expression,
to black artists, musicians, entertainers who came,
or were discovered here before achieving fame,
when nowhere else America would open the door
to them due to prejudice based on their color.

Harlem, determined not to let black talents
go wasted because of racial intolerance,
nurtured these blessings and gifts like gold
and enjoyed and reveled in them until the world
realized talent was talent regardless of color
and rushed uptown after the midnight hour
to taste what they were missing in Jim Crow's world,
to be enchanted in this magical new world.
They flocked to the Savoy on Saturday night
to stomp to the best jazz music in sight,
to dance the Big Apple, the rhumboogie,
the lindy hop, peckin, and the shimmy,
or to watch mambo dancing and the jitterbug jive,
and the flying Charleston comes alive
at the Savoy, "the Home of Happy Feet,"
where they danced on the 'track' never missing a beat
with two live bands taking turns until dawn --
Chick Webb, Count Basie, Louis Armstrong,
Fletcher Henderson, Erskin Hawkins, and so on --
white people 'went crazy' in a black town.

Just a block away, the Cotton Club was near.
This was Harlem, but Cotton wouldn't let races mix there
'less you're passing white, or you're one of the band
or you're a performer, or you're a hired hand.

But white folks wouldn't go to the real Harlem hangouts,
the four-story walk-ups, and see what partying is about
in the throbbing rent parties on a Saturday night,
nor to other pay parties where jazz was out of sight,
where Willie the Lion and Fats Waller tickled piano all night.
Beneath the Savoy was the Vaudeville Comedy Club crowd,
an after-hour place where no whites were allowed,
where friends and jazz players went after work to hang out
and hear Bessie Smith as she is belting out:
"I'm goin' to start walking 'cause I got a wooden pair of shoes.
Goin' to keep walking 'till I lose these sobbin'–hearted blues."
Yes, Harlem was swinging at night, and whites seemed to be nice,
but in daylight, it was still far from interracial paradise.

In the nineteen twenties, the most popular location,
where the hottest music and jazz clubs were found,
was on Lenox Avenue, a way uptown.
There were other clubs, too: Connie's Inn with a nice beat
on Seventh Avenue and one Thirty-first Street
(for whites only); and Small's Paradise on Seventh Avenue
and one thirty-fifth -- Malcolm once worked there, too.
But the bulk of the action was on Lenox Avenue
with the Savoy Ballroom, with the Cotton Club,
the Lenox Lounge and some after-hour jazz clubs.

In the famous jazz clubs, you went to listen to
talents like Duke Ellington, creator of Mood Indigo,
Take the "A" Train, Don't Mean a Thing, just a few
of his works too many to list; Harlem was his venue.
And there, too, the creator of Hi Di Ho and his band,
Cab Calloway, zoot suits and all was quite a showman.
Also, Count Basie, band leader, one of the best in his prime
who won nine Grammies to prove it for all time;
and James Price Johnson, creator of stride piano style
and his famous **Charleston.** He taught Fats Waller for a while.
And there was Lil Hardin, jazz pianist wife of Louis Armstrong,
who died while playing a live concert honoring Louis Armstrong.

These are a few of the famous jazz musicians
who performed at the jazz clubs during the Renaissance,
also entertainers like Lena Horne, with her beauty and songs,
who thrilled the Cotton Club, and Bill "Bojangles" Robinson
who could tap dance anyone off the stage dancing
to thunderous applause, though the only sad thing
was blacks were not allowed though they could dance
and perform there and work as hired hands.

Another place not on Lenox Avenue,
two ten one eighteenth street near Seventh Avenue,
where to hear Bebop jam sessions, you had to go,
was Minton's Playhouse, a jazz club that was so
sizzling! Though the food was good, it was the jamming
that was the greatest! The place was cramming
to hear the best jazz musicians on the planet ever,
the likes of Dizzy Gillespie, Charlie Parker,
the genius of Thelonius Monk, Charlie Christian,
the sounds of Coleman Hawkins, Don Byas, and
Roy Eldridge, Miles Davis, and Lester Young,
and no slouch on sax was Henry Minton.

Monday night was musicians' night off,
called Celebrity Night when the gloves came off
and they all were there jazzing and jamming,
and you had to be there to hear bebop slamming.
Minton's was the hottest jazz spot in town;
Minton's was the place where Bebop was born.
But in the late nineteen sixties, as everything goes,
Minton's declined, and it eventually closed.

Another famous social gathering place
where sculptors, writers, actors graced
and were royally entertained "The Dark Tower,"
owned by Madam C. J. Walker and A'Lelia, her daughter,
was a converted floor in their one thirty-sixth street
townhouse near Lenox, which was lavishly replete.
I could not speak about Harlem's bright era,
without a mention of C. J. and A'Lelia.

Long before there was Oprah Winfrey,
shortly after the turn of the twentieth century,
at the dawn of the Harlem Renaissance,
when her story defied all the odds of chance,
there was the one and only Madam C. J. Walker,
born Sarah Breedlove, a poor cotton picker,
daughter of ex-slaves, washerwoman, kitchen scrubber,
who, with a dollar fifty and a dream about hair care,
became the first self-made female millionaire.
She built a mansion in Irvington, Villa Lewaro,
to rival Jay Gould's and the Rockefellers next door.
By her death in nineteen nineteen, she had built
a factory, hired thousands of blacks and willed
that her hair-care company be run by black women.
A well-known philanthropist for black causes, she even
engaged in protests for black empowerment,
and was a patron for artists during the Renaissance movement.
Her daughter, A'Lelia, continued in her name
during the black renaissance, and she gained fame
hosting black writers artists at lavish parties,
"The Joy Goddess of Harlem's Nineteen Twenties,"
said Langston Hughes, who wrote "For A'Lelia,"
a poem that was read on her funeral day
in nineteen thirty-one. But for her famous mother,
a commemorative stamp was issued in her honor.

To Harlem, the migrants brought religion, too,
for religion had sustained them and gotten them through
slavery and Jim Crow, and it would sustain them now.
Harlem had more than four hundred churches somehow,
Methodists, Baptists, Catholics, Episcopalians,
black synagogues, African-Mehodist-Episcopalians.
Abyssinian Baptist Church I'll especially mention
because it was, and still is, a famous congregation.
Its roots trace back to eighteen hundred-eight
when some visiting Ethiopian merchants became irate,
along with Afro-Americans who were attending
a white Baptist Church downtown where racial seating

caused them to leave angry and to form a new congregation
called The Abyssinian Baptist Church, with Afro orientation,
inspired by the African nation of Abyssinia,
that today is referred to as the country of Ethiopia.
They first moved to Anthony Street (renamed Worth Street),
then they moved to Waverly Place, which could not meet
the size and needs of a growing congregation.
As Harlem became black, they decided to move uptown
which would markedly increase the size of their congregation.
They appointed a new pastor in nineteen hundred eight
named Adam Clayton Powell, Sr., and did not have long to wait
until tithing and offerings covered the bill
for a new church as fine as money could build,
of Gothic and Tudor style, marble furnishings, stain glass windows
at their present location where they opened its doors
in nineteen twenty-three on West one thirty-eight Street.

It was a Black people's church that looked very neat!
Since then, the pastor's title passed to his son's capable hands,
a most eloquent orator and U.S. congressman,
Adam Clayton Powell Jr., a Civil Rights champion,
who led many protests and demonstrations,
against businesses that wouldn't hire blacks,
and picketed the World's Fair till they hired hundreds of blacks.
He worked tirelessly to relieve the poor in Harlem,
for which Emperor Haile Selassie honored him.

His greatest work came when elected to Congress,
in nineteen forty-five, and with two fingers, no less,
you could count the number of black congressmen,
serving in the United States Congress back then.
He gave hell to the Southern segregationists,
and the gang of entrenched white supremacists,
and when he became chair of a powerful committee,
the Education and Labor, with his seniority
he achieved forty-eight pieces of major legislation,
that helped black people. He was a champion.
Not one bill could pass without a "Powell Amendment,"
that benefited his Afro-American constituents.
He was hated for it, and his enemies, by conspiracy,
stripped his chairmanship of the E & L Committee
but could not remove him from Congress. They tried to,
but that the electorate alone had the power to do.
In nineteen seventy, he lost the Democratic primary,
and in nineteen seventy-two, he died in Bimini.
His most famous phrase was, "Keep the faith, Baby."
A monument was erected in his honor in Harlem,
and a state building and street were named after him.
Other capable pastors followed, and the church became
one of the largest congregations of worldwide fame.

There were Christian cultists like George Wilson Becton,
who in nineteen thirty-three, for some unknown reason
was shot to death – a still unsolved case.
And there was Bishop Charles Manuel "Daddy Grace,"
who was the founder of the United House of Prayer.
He became well known almost everywhere
as a flamboyant and self-proclaimed Messiah,
but he was neither a bishop nor was he a Messiah.
It is said he once claimed he gave God a vacation,
and he told his faithful congregation,
if they sinned against God, Daddy Grace will save them;
but if they sinned against Grace, not even God can save them.
He preached and practiced generosity to the poor
and did a lot of community projects and more.
He was a very charismatic leader, claiming,
the power to do miraculous faith healing.

Nonetheless, through investments and capable management
in business and real estate in Harlem and the continent,
He built up a prosperous religious organization,
that has many branches throughout the nation,
and, even long after his death in nineteen sixty,
it continued to prosper from investments in the community.

But perhaps the greatest cultist ever
was Father Divine, referred to as the Messenger,
who claimed he was God, which his followers swore him to be.
He was a student of "The New Thought" philosophy,
but he preached his own doctrine, for he was divine,
and he had over two million followers in his prime.
He preached to his followers to renounce personal property,
to live by a strict moral code, and practice celibacy.
He banned alcohol and tobacco, called his followers "angels,"
and regarded as unimportant any and all details
of his worldly existence; therefore, no one knew
where and when he was born and whom to.
He required the members to donate all their worldly
possessions to the Mission, which made them, collectively,
a very prosperous organization
when you add up investments throughout the nation.
Father Divine was known to be honest,
and devoted to his followers. At best
he allowed himself just a few luxuries:
He lived in the finest of the Mission's properties,
was chauffeured in a brand-new Rolls Royce and, to boot,
was always dressed in a fine three-piece suit.

Back in nineteen fifteen, when he, with some followers,
was chased out of Georgia for claiming to have God's powers,
and for being thought a nuisance bordering on insane,
poor people still believed in him and praised his name.
He moved to Sayville, New York, and bought a house,
and by nineteen twenty-nine, he was already famous
for feeding the poor, helping them find employment,
and pooling their resources to make wise investments.
Each Sunday at his house, he featured an all-day banquet,
free of charge and open to anyone who wanted to attend.
Word quickly spread of this bounty from Heaven,
and all the poor people, mostly blacks, did attend.

White residents of Sayville, though, didn't like this invasion
and had him arrested as a nuisance to the town.
After they conducted a thorough police investigation,
they found no improprieties at all at the Peace Mission.
But Divine was still sentenced to one year in prison
by a judge who called him a fraud for no reason.
When that judge promptly died three days later,
Divine's reputation soared higher and higher.
Like Jesus, he had been wrongly accused,
and his persecutor paid in full for this abuse.
Divine was freed on bail, and in a week or two,
his conviction was overturned, and the Peace Mission grew.
After this, he moved his headquarters to Harlem, and
that helped his movement to rapidly expand.

It had now reached its height, "The Peace Mission;"
but in nineteen thirty-seven, a setback was brought on
when a former disciple sued him and his peers
for money, she gave them over the years.
A long court case ended in a ruling against him,
which could have meant his financial ruin,
if all ex-devotees should also sue him,
but Father and Mother Divine did some praying,
and won their appeal; although five years later,
another court reviewed and reopened the matter,
and ordered him to pay, which resulted in a draw,
for the Great One moved to Philly and escaped the law.
And since State laws forbade serving subpoenas on Sunday,
he often spoke on Sabbath days in Harlem anyway.
In the nineteen forties, his principle of celibacy
and frugal collective living were gradually
losing their appeal, the organization stagnating,
Father Divine retired to a life of quiet living
on his Woodmont Estate, Gladwyne, Pa. 'till his death
In nineteen sixty-five, he departed from earth
and still, no one knows the secret of his birth.

Another movement, one that was non-Christian,
known as the Black Muslim Nation of Islam,
under its second leader, the Honorable Elijah Muhammad,
and his gifted protégé, Minister Malcolm X, had
a marked effect on the souls of black men
and youth, especially, who lived in Harlem.
It gave them a sense of pride and dignity
and taught black people to control their own destiny.
Beginning with the year nineteen hundred fifty-two
to the year nineteen hundred sixty-four, it grew,
thanks primarily to Malcolm X's preaching.
With his speeches, he tore down every brick and pillar
and every false logic and argument racists could muster,
and in so doing, exposed the very foundation
of Jim Crow with eloquence and perfect diction.
He put fear into oppressors as no black man
had ever done before, with truth at his command.
He was like an answer to millions of black prayers,
and he could not be bought or moved by naysayers.
Yes, without a doubt, and his enemies knew,
he was a champion, incorruptible, too.
He was the reason for the movement attracting,
almost a hundred thousand and was still growing,
but the signs that were there he could not escape,
when the flawed meets the flawless and truth is at stake.
So Malcolm X, in the end, had to break from the movement.
Some people believe that the truth is one element,
like his flawless principles that caused his doom,
when one evening in the ill-fated Audubon ballroom
he was assassinated by a gang of far lesser men,
and from that day, like a curse, never again
would the Black Muslim movement be the same.
But the great freedom fighter, Malcolm X, will always be
a hero and a champion to the black community.

In the early part of the great migration
when Harlem was transitioning to a black population,
and the whites who were there started moving out,
the fancy homes and residences, no doubt,
became occupied by blacks who had the means,
and celebrity status that goes with the scenes.
Sugar Hill, for example, overlooking Manhattan,
and looking out into the valley of Harlem,
with its fine brownstones and architecture,
was a choice of celebrities and people with stature
such as Duke Ellington, Thurgood Marshall, Count Basie,
W.E.B. DuBois, Kenneth Clark, James A. Bailey.

Between Seventh and Eighth Avenues on one Thirty-ninth Street
in the middle of Harlem that you cannot miss it,
was another section that rich white folks built
for their elegant living before they could imagine it
would become a black town. This was Striver's Row,
three rows of townhouses, just so you'd know,
with gated alleys originally for horses and carriages
but now offer private parking like in private garages.
Its elegant, unified facades gave the impression,
that these houses were small, elegant mansions.
Originally called the King Model Houses
after its developer, David King. These houses
are recognized as architectural gems.
Many famous residents have lived in them,
such as Eubie Blake, Fletcher Henderson,
Stepin Fetchit, Bill Bojangles Robinson,
Adam Clayton Powell, Jr., W. C. Handy,
Scott Joplin, Henry Pace, and Vertner Tandy.

Between one forty-ninth Street and one-fiftieth Street,
seventh and eighth avenues on the block complete,
was built another group of houses above par
known as the Dunbar Apartments after Paul Laurence Dunbar.
A historic site, it was built in nineteen twenty-six,
to relieve at the time a growing housing crisis.

It was originally intended as a middle-class development
and the first large garden complex for Harlem residents.
With six buildings and five hundred-eleven apartments,
it was the first large cooperative with mortgage payments.
After twenty-two years, tenants would own it outright.
It was listed by New York City as an historic site.
The rest of Harlem was regular tenement housing,
which meant, in most cases, overcrowding.

There was so much talent in Harlem in those days
just starving and being neglected, which would amaze,
but it took foresight and a venue in which to present,
and display this black talent and entertainment.
A burlesque house on One Twenty-Fifth Street was shorn
of its out-of-place character and quickly transformed
to a showtime theater that was named the Apollo.
In nineteen thirty-four, it was the place for blacks to go.
It was opened with a colored review, "Jazz a la Carte,"
featuring the well-known Ralph Cooper, Benny Carter,
his orchestra, and sixteen show-stoppers. It was the only
theater at the time to hire blacks in New York City.

From its beginning, the Apollo sponsored amateur shows
hosted by Ralph Cooper, and there was exposed
the best young black talent. Countless stars were born,
and legends were made after they performed,
and thrilled the crowds at that historic theater,
like a seventeen-year-old who became later,
"Lady Ella," who made her debut there,
and launched her distinguished singing career
in nineteen thirty-four when she won first prize
on Amateur Night, which was no surprise.
Among other outstanding black artists
who launched their careers at the Apollo, here's a list:
James Brown, Stevie Wonder, Billie Holiday,
Gladys Knight and the Pips, Sarah Vaughn, Marvin Gaye,
The Jackson Five, Luther Vandross, Ben E. King,
Patti La Belle, Maria Carey, Aretha Franklin.
Old-time favorites who wowed the gallery
were Dewey "Pigmeat," Markham, and Johnny Lee.

With the rise in the black population, thanks to employment
opportunities and the Great Migration, it was evident
when greedy landlords were overcharging black tenants,
that blacks would face hardships one day, paying such rents.
By the fifties, moreover, there was impending doom,
due to high unemployment and crime in place of boom,
and old grievances and tensions that only got worse.
A trend was when things got bad, blacks were the first,
to be fired and feel there's no fairness nor security,
for them anywhere in this society.
So, when the fifties brought turbulence and social unrest,
in the form of riots, strikes, and civil protests,
throughout the country, you could have bet,
that Harlem, too, would be in the thick of it
with rent strikes by tenants under Jesse Gray,
protests by the Congress of Racial Equality,
the National Urban League, HARYOU, and
cries for black independence by the Nation of Islam.

In the South, nonviolent groups were being led by
Reverend Dr. Martin Luther King, Jr., who gained high
respect in Harlem for fighting for civil rights.
All pent-up grievances in the country came to light
and as a result of these struggles in the fifties and sixties,
Civil rights laws were passed to address injustices,
though the cost was high, for we lost Dr. King and Malcolm
who gave their lives fighting for black people's freedom.

Harlem had to pay the price, for change had to come,
so the wheels could turn and time could move on.
It seems after its best days came and went,
no amount of Urban Renewal with good intent
could reverse its inevitable decline and decay.
Some say that it was planned that way,
but the unnatural manner of its growth, to begin with,
and short-lived existence were easy to predict.
Furthermore, facing overcrowding, neglect, disillusionment,
most people's will and desires were largely spent.

Circumstances forced many blacks to move out
and condemned and abandoned buildings were boarded shut.
Anyway, seasons come and go, transitions as well,
But, then, that's for scholars of history to tell.
By the late nineteen hundreds, only a skeleton remained
of the great town of Harlem, which will never be the same.

If you should walk the streets of Harlem today
and meet some ghosts who lived in its heyday,
they wouldn't recognize it. I wonder what they'd say,
when they saw the dying and all the decay
of what was once a proud and booming town,
where black identity broke new ground
when countless black people made Harlem their home,
where black art and culture came into its own,
where the black writer, philosopher, and thinker transformed
black literature and thought, and the Renaissance was born,
where the culture of musical art was transformed
by black originality, unfettered by any white norm,
where no taboo or brainwashing could hold down
the desire for freedom and human expression.

Lately, I've seen many buildings being torn down,
and I've seen new buildings rising up from the ground
that does not look like black people's homes,
high rises with price tags for the rich alone.
Harlem was once a place in transition,
during the Great Black Northern Migration,
and now it is going through another transition,
a transition more properly called gentrification,
bringing in a different kind of population.
But the Harlem that was once here for a season
and made its mark with the muses' pen,
we will never see that Harlem again.

Blues for Harlem
(1980)

Harlem, at the turn of the 20th century, was the densest 3 square miles of humanity anywhere in America due to the northern migration of black people from the south. Between 1919 and 1935, it became Harlem for the ages. It fulfilled the yearnings in Black people's souls for freedom. Harlem was where the creative, intellectual, literary, imaginative, musical, artistic, spiritual, messianic outpourings of all the genius that black people possessed came together in the fulfillment and launching of a true rebirth of the human spirit. It was a golden age... that was what Harlem during this period represented. Sadly, though, as spectacular as were its birth and life, tragic was Harlem's demise. It was a golden age that could not last, whose glory days came quickly and passed into the ages. The Blues was an art form that was one of its own and, appropriately, the name of this poem.

The memory of Harlem is like the blues,
like a sad, sad song within a song
of joy and sadness, all diffused
in the ashes of time that's come and gone,
to be sung now by the muse.

It is like a kind of haunting blues,
a soulful, haunting, taunting blues
that, for a spell, played high notes here
with so much heartache and flare,
then disappeared.

It was black people's love affair
with hopes, yearnings, aspirations here,
struggling to find a "dream deferred,"
too long till their strong voices were heard
unmuted and undeterred.

'T was like a tide held back too long
by wrongs whose final day had come,
whose barriers came tumbling down
like the walls of Jericho had done,
when Black people stopped turning around.

This place called Harlem was bestowed
with a new spirit, a fire that glowed,
and so much talent and genius that flowed
like a river from black people's souls,
Once the dam was broken, they took control

of their aspirations and destiny, God knows.
Once the chains were broken that caused their woes,
black souls would never be the same
and would not settle for chains again.
That was, to me, the sweet refrain

that filled the air in Harlem's days,
when the word brother or sister meant what it says.
It was truly a rising up for a season,
and black people's voices taught the world a lesson,
that this was the age of black courage and reason;

that this was the golden age of Harlem
when Black people had a new song, a new rhythm,
that this was the age when a New Negro had risen
and a new voice brought a new black radicalism
to the struggle for equality against racism;

that this was the golden age of Harlem
when Black people played a new song, a new rhythm.
O sing me that song, O sing me that song
that was the gift called Harlem, now come and gone,
now faded away just like a phantom.

When you walk the streets now, at times you can hear
an echo as if the ghosts are still there,
the heroes and leaders, the thinkers and fighters,
the dreamers and poets, the artists and writers,
the teachers, preachers, soul brothers, and sisters.

Many gathering places on the avenues
have changed, but sometimes there are clues.
All of the sites where events once took place
are now torn down or have a different face.
You had to know Harlem, in any case.

The memory, to some, is like the blues,
like a sad, sad song within a song
of joy and sadness now diffused
in the ashes of time that's come and gone,
but still remains just like the blues.

The Souls of Black People Are a River (1964)

O sons and daughters, precious children,
uprooted from your native lands,
taken from family, loved ones, friends
like helpless quarry against your will,
shackled and packed like grain and beef
in stench-filled and in creaking holds
of straining cargo ships bound for
ports distant, if you survived and sold
like beasts of burden or common flesh
in marketplaces to the highest bidders.

Then, from vile trading marts shipped off
again to final destinations,
to killing fields, slave camps, plantations
and other fields and forms of servitude.
You knew not where you were being taken,
only that it was far from home
forever, to die as slaves, as things,
as beasts of burden doomed to hard labor.

O sons and daughters, in grief and chains
from dungeons to dungeons, horrors to horrors,
in bestial conditions, yoked like dumb brutes,
forced to journey over bitter trails,
butchered and martyred along the way;
hell knew no terror worse than those
they used to break your bodies and wills,
to bruise and brutalize your souls!

O sons and daughters, you've borne so much
in many lands across the earth
for centuries, wherever your seeds
were spread—by evil forces dispersed—
yet ceasing never, forever yearning,
to find that place where you belong;
even in your songs, your spirituals,
the theme was always 'returning home.'

O sons and daughters, not one day passes
under the yoke of unrighteousness,
under the scourge of injustices
that you do not bleed, cut down like dogs
by those who stalk you in shadows, in streets,
who see you still as 'chattel' slaves
and not God's children with sacred rights
of life, liberty, and equality.

O sons and daughters, you bear no shame;
guilt is not yours in Judgment's court;
and if you feel a longing for
that which was taken from you, it is
your soul seeking for answers from
its source—the mother of all mankind
whose nurturing soul was always linked
to yours throughout time, wherever you've been.

O Mother of mothers, your precious blood
was bled like a river that flowed outward
into many dark and desperate places,
through the flesh of your flesh abducted
to distant lands not of their birth
and planted there against their will,
and robbed of their identity
and branded as others' property.

O dearest Mother of Mankind, were you
to send out a mother's cry to all
your children and their children's children
all over the world today, there be
weeping and wailing, and robbers would quake
and slavers, evildoers would flee when they hear
such a mother's anguish for the pain
and suffering her children have endured.

The souls of black people are a river,
a river that flows from the first womb incarnate,
birthed in the cradle of the Garden of Eden
where life first began upon the earth.
Like all your children, I came from you
and deep, deep down within my soul
I feel a longing that binds me to you,
O Mother of mothers of all mankind.

On Reading About the Lynching of a Black Man

The point of this poem is self-evident in the last stanza. (1968)

I was reading an old news story
that was O so grim and gory!
It told how they lynched a black man,
imagine if you can!

They gagged and bound him tight
in the middle of the night,
crackers, honkies, redneck trash
flailing hatred with the lash!

Jiggers, such a coward's night,
Klansmen dressed in hoods of white!
Murder, murder in their sight,
could not even stand the light!

They tortured, showed him no mercy!
Hanged him high up on a tree!
Then I thought of Calvary—
and Christ who died upon a tree.

MS In a Bottle
(1972)

I am going to write a letter
which I'll place inside a bottle—
a manuscript in a bottle—
about this world and things I've seen.
I'll seal it, and I'll set it on
an ocean that flows throughout time!

Then, if someone in the future time
should chance upon my manuscript,
I hope the world is different then.
I hope there are no boundaries,
no more barriers of any kind
to separate humanity!

No guarded borders on this earth,
no states or countries to fight for,
no wars, no treaties, armies, guns,
no segregated neighborhoods,
no social classes, poverty,
no racial biases or codes!

Perhaps people will call themselves
brothers and sisters, too, at last,
and trust will be a way of life,
and hate will be a word removed
from all the dictionaries,
and from the human heart!

If someone in a future time
should find my bottled manuscript,
perhaps they should not read it, though,
for reading it, they will be shocked
to learn what kind of beings lived,
hated and killed each other, so,
a long, long time ago!

Prison Walls
(1977)

"Prison walls are made of skin,"
some say, "and cannot be erased!
Depending on which skin you're in,
it's hell you're bound to face!"

But I believe we brand the skin
only because it's there!
Real prison walls lie deep within,
they're made of *hate* and *fear*.

How many prisoners are there?
Why, all of us! You see,
we never even bother
to see that none of us is free!

We all live in our prisons,
and don't even mind the cold,
and make up many reasons
to barricade the soul.

So many years of hating
have left a trail of shame,
of senseless human wasting
in this Republic's name.

Yet, we go on pretending
that some of us are free;
and keep the cauldrons boiling
with hate for you and me!

It isn't any wonder
jails flourish in our time
when you and I surrender
to one another's crime.

We made our prisons very strong,
yet it is not too late
to break the walls and barriers down
and rid ourselves of hate.

Tear down your jail, earth brother,
and help me tear down mine!
Let us free one another
and wipe the slate of time.

The Painting on a Wall

(In the year 1964, a few months after the Baptist church bombing in Birmingham, Alabama, by the KKK that killed four innocent little black girls, an artist painted the face of a beautiful black child that he wanted to represent or evoke symbolically the sadness for those victims. He painted the face against a dark velvet background on a framed canvas and hung it on a wall in this public bar. This is not only for the tragedy of those four children, the painter said, but he wanted to portray the tragedy of all black children in racist America. One of the most striking features of the painting was a continuous stream of crystal teardrops flowing down the cheeks from both eyes of the little girl! Those were teardrops that inspired the writer who was sitting on a bar stool when he wrote this poem.):

Teardrops bright and clear,
crystals of despair,
sparkle in the dim light's glare
from the corners of dark eyes
like they're questions in disguise,

flowing and yet lingering there
like a stain of some disgrace
that the darkness can't erase,
like a soul's bitter lament
for a promise cruelly rent!

Teardrops bright and clear
fill the silence now unbroken
like a phrase that's never spoken,
like a tragedy reflected
in an image introjected!

Teardrops in the dim light's glare
cry out to this cold, harsh place
where hate shrouds the human race,
where injustice rears its head
each day and is richly fed!

Teardrops bright and clear
like a sadness that is seen
for the dreams that might have been,
for the hopes dashed to despair
in a world that does not care!

Teardrops bright and clear,
blemishes that sorrow paints
in the shadows of restraints
that can never wash away
though the canvas may decay,

for the tears that are seen there
flow within the eternal breast
where they'll never be suppressed,
where God's justice does not sleep
and rivers run dark and deep.

Ode to a Freedom Fighter

Dedicated to Dr. Martin Luther King, Jr. (written in 1968)

1
The phantom world has gained a noble prize!
High in its martyred ranks has been inscribed
his name who now, along with patriarchs, lies!
How rightly might his followers have proscribed
Death claiming him were it their power to choose!
But who are we to stay the reaper's hand?
Mere mortals, proud at best, but mortals still.
Though we might wish, we cannot Death abuse
nor stay its hand, only the Maker can –
for all things work according to His will.

2
Death looked at him one day and, envious, said,
"Live briefly now, brave heart, but come tomorrow
a bitter path awaits where you must tread,
and where you'll go, no mortal flesh can follow!"
"Why?" Earth lamented when in silent pause
it mourned the light taken that meant so much,
a light that shone so brightly in our lives!
Earth grieved its loss, perplexed by Heaven's cause.
Too cruel seemed Death's sudden, awful touch
that somehow we forgot a dream survives!

3
Is he dead? No, no, banish baneful despair!
His spirit walks among the living still.
Wherever oppressed are gathered, he is there!
See how he rises to his feet to quell
a restless multitude that's standing by
awaiting! Now—be still! Hush! Hear him speak!
"Let freedom ring," he cries, "let freedom ring!
The dream! The dream! You must not let it die!
From every valley, every mountain peak
on earth, let freedom ring, let freedom ring!"

The Bravest Warrior

(Dedicated to Minister Malcolm X, the bravest, truest warrior who did not
hesitate to die for his people.)
1964

He took the cup of knowledge, drank deeply,
and was instilled with truth and wisdom,
then he emerged from the dungeons of darkness
with a new calling: a quest for freedom.

Armed with wisdom and truth, he came,
never again would he be a slave;
he was prepared to do battle, a warrior
destined to fight or to sleep in his grave!

Glowing in the light like a fiery prophet,
he was a tall, shining, brave black warrior
piercing the air with his voice like the thunder,
echoing a pledge never to surrender

to the forces of hypocrisy,
to the authors of his people's pain,
to the robbers, brainwashers, oppressors,
to the slavers who forged his chains!

And as he spoke on so many occasions,
every black, young and old, stood up tall;
his was the voice of black manhood, a nation,
his was the spirit of blacks one and all!

When he spoke, they knew a prayer was answered:
He was an instrument playing the right chord.
Black youth responded and anxiously gathered
poised like an army ready to go forward.

He led the way, and the young blood they followed!
How he struck terror in the hearts of oppressors!
He shook the very foundation they hallowed,
exposed their myths while inspiring his followers;

and, as the smoke grew thick in battle,
his enemies plotted to silence his voice;
but when a warrior goes into battle,
He faces danger without any choice!

So he went forward as only he could –
Nothing would alter the mission he bore,
for he belonged to the people, the struggle,
and he resigned to what lay in store.

If you have seen a braver man, tell me!
Nothing could deter his course anymore;
so in the shadows, when Death stalked him
he came forth dressed in his shining armor!

Never was he more in his power,
never a warrior glittered more brightly
as he confronted his final hour!
Even against Death, he stood tall and mighty!

If the oppressors, the killers of men,
thought with their bullets to silence this man,
thought they could silence the hopes of a people,
when will they learn that they never can?

O vain oppressors and killers of men,
something you never could understand:
Though you may kill again and again,
the spirit of Malcolm lives in every man!

Song of The Man from Alkebu-lan
1982

I am a Black man; who are you?
Are you a Black man, too?
They have tried hard to erase
memories my ancestors placed
in my spirit, in my bosom,
in my soul and in my song.
Though my culture was arrested,
it is still here manifested
in my sinews and my brain,
in my blood in every vein.

I am a black man, yes, and proud,
made of spirit, flesh, and blood
mixed with sun, enriched by earth,
the dawn of time witnessed my birth.
There are those who scorn and fear me
and they chained me and enslaved me.
Though my flesh was scarred and shackled,
and my manhood bruised and battered,
something deep in me rebels
and, despite all, proudly swells.

If you ask me, "What did you do
why so much was done to you?"
It is not I who must answer
for the yoke, I've labored under,
for the cruel subjugation,
for the wanton degradation,
for being stripped of my own name,
forced to mock myself in shame,
copy someone else's image
while they scorned my heritage.

I am a Black man, vanquished never,
son of Alkebu-lan forever,
changed, maybe, since slave ships landed,
but I'll always be reminded
Alkebu-lan is in my soul
and alone can make me whole.
My 'black' blood drenched on this shore
gave it nurture and much more;
still, I struggle for my freedom
and my place within the sun.

I am a Black man, scorned, reviled,
I am a Black man from the Nile,
I am a Black man from the Congo,
and the regions of the Limpopo,
I am from mountain and valley,
I am from the banks of Zambezi
and the shores washed by the Niger,
son of Alkebu-lan forever.
My true heritage, richly blessed,
is the source of my blackness.

Son of ancient wealth and wisdom
that predates all Christendom,
deep within my proud black bosom
I can hear a distant drum!
Even as its fury rages
from the ashes of past ages,
in it is a bond that binds me
to my ancestors where they may be,
to the roots from which I sprang:
Alkebu-lan! Alkebu-lan!

I Was Stranded Late One Night in New York City 1978

(This was the other side of midnight that I did not want to see, another failure, another guilt, another blight that makes a mockery of society. Who is to blame for these creatures that roam the night?)

I was stranded late one night in New York City
with nowhere to go, and the scenes were not pretty.
By then, most New Yorkers were locked in for the night,
and shadows concealed alley cats out of sight.
Wall Street looked like a graveyard zone,
Delancey and Court Streets' hustle-bustle were gone,
Broadway playhouses had closed for the night,
and Lincoln Center crowds had taken flight.
Most shops and stores were closed in the city,
and the usually hectic Port Authority
and Penn Station bustle had come to a hush,
and the booths were shut down till the morning rush.

The subways were running but were far in between;
The night air and darkness enveloped the scene.
The hour was between midnight and twilight of morning,
and the good citizens lay in their beds, snoring;
but outside, the denizens of the dark night were seen;
outside a world of the living dead reigned supreme,
a world of the wretched, the damned, the castoffs,
the hopelessly tainted, the wasted, the lost,
the desperate, the broken in spirit and mind,
an anti- or sub-world of yours and mine,
a world of creatures cuddled in corners in the cold,
sprawled on benches, creeping, crawling out from some hole,
a world of empty glances, pitiful stares,
of haggard looks and of raggedy wares,
of swollen and often of rotting flesh,
a world of zombies with the smell of dead fish
roaming in the night air in a bottomless pit
where the lower the level, a level is beneath it,
a world of lost souls ghoulishly surviving,
being victims more than victimizing.

A world where all Christian laws are dead,
where the laws are the laws of the jungle instead,
a world where human values do not count,
where up is down, and down is out,
a world with its codes that are different than ours,
where the fear's not of darkness but of daylight hours,
a world wherein kindness is an ugly word,
where a gift is suspicious and a giver absurd,
where brutality itself seems a generous thing
if instead of being maimed, the victim stops breathing.

Though busy New Yorkers' workday was done,
and they slept, most of them snugly bedded down,
the guilt of humanity could not sleep,
the guilt of humanity was walking the street,
up and down Times Square, Forty-second Street,
Eighth Avenue, Broadway, the Port Authority beat,
Penn Station, the West Side, the East Side, along the Square,
Harlem, uptown, downtown, everywhere,
flaking, flicking, tricking, cruising along,
snorting, shooting whatever they get their hands on,
aimless, mindless, without feeling or fears,
groping, scratching, dying, and nobody cares,
killing, stealing, shooting junk in their veins
in the bottomless pit where the living dead reign.

Yes, New Yorkers were safely locked in for the night,
and shadows concealed alley cats out of sight,
but the guilt of humanity was not asleep;
the guilt of humanity was walking the street.

The Great Enigma

(America The Beautiful?)

There is a land built on the premise
"All men are created equal";
but that land fulfills not promise
of the burning lamp on a pedestal.

There is a land called democracy
where God's words: "Love one another"
are twisted by hypocrisy
to exclude the darker brother.

There is a land that preaches justice,
brotherhood, love, Christianity;
but in that land, they do not practice
what they preach to humanity.

There is a land claiming to be truly
a beacon for all seeking to breathe freely;
yet it treats so many unjustly,
denying them equality.

There is a land of fertile fields
harvesting from tarnished seeds;
and in that land of high ideals
they mock God with bitter deeds.

The sins of all men, great and small,
cannot escape the chastening rod!
On Judgment Day, when they are called,
how will they face and answer God?

"DID YOU LOVE ONE ANOTHER?
DID YOU TREAT EACH OTHER JUSTLY?
DID YOU LOVE YOUR DARKER BROTHER
AND EMBRACE HIM EQUALLY?"

They will stand before the throne,
and try to say they loved the Lord;
but their deeds were written in stone,
and their hearts untrue to God's word.

Then, by their guilt, God shall so order:
"DEPART FROM ME, I KNOW YOU NOT!
I WAS YOUR DARKER BROTHER;
YOU SCORNED ME, AND YOU LOVED ME NOT."

This Is My Song For Humanity

We marvel at the same blue sky,
the same bright stars, you and I,
the same old universe above;

We breathe in and out the same air,
drink the water from the same hydrosphere,
and reap from the same soil that we love.

We share the same bright sunlight,
the same darkness, same gift of sight;
hear the same thunder, see the same rainbows.

We dream the same dreams, hope for the same things:
a better life for us, our loved ones, and fledglings;
and feel the same joys and sorrows.

We are driven by the same thirsts and fears;
feel the same pains, shed the same tears;
are driven by the same hunger and longings;

We wonder where we came from, why we are here,
where we are going and what we'll find there
and whether our past lives have meaning.

We count the same blessings and go to church.
We keep searching for answers since our birth
and find that with answers more questions abound.

We pray to the same God, rest when weary,
measure our days that fly by just as quickly
and by the time we start counting, they are all gone.

What is it that makes us different, then?
That is the question that racks my brain.
Are we really so different, as some of us claim?

Or is it that, if we accept such a claim,
the difference is our outer garment of shame?
Somehow, it's a dilemma I cannot explain.

Except to say we can blame one thing:
If we take a good look under the skin
There's a mischievous protein called melanin.

Why you have so little and I so much, to begin,
is because of Mother Nature's conditioning
the human species to the climate they live in

Thousands and thousands of years, literally.
So, the truth is white and black skin identity
used by modern man is an absurdity.

If everything was one color, there'd be no beauty!
And I don't think the world could exist that way,
where there was no color variety.

We'd hate each other out of boredom more than shame
if we all looked identically the same;
and not even Mother Nature would play that game

with only one kind of flower with no color
or one shade of specie and no other,
with everything looking exactly the same.

If we can look in a garden and see how beauty
comes in all shapes and colors painted magnificently,
Why can't we see the same with humanity?

Furthermore, our spirits and souls that we cannot see
with the naked eye, they all, honestly,
are colorless with the same destiny.

So, doesn't that make us unequivocally
brothers and sisters since originally
we all came from the same human family?

I Am A Dreamer

I am a dreamer,
a dreamer of justice and human rights,
a dreamer of righting wrongs,
and I was dreaming:
What if the world were color blind
and the myth of 'race' was no more?
Would we all join in a "kumbaya"
holding hands with love in unity?
Or would we still discriminate
and hate each other and segregate?
What would it be like if no more
we called each other black or white
and all of us looked just alike?
It could not be that pigment, then –
or lack of it – would seal our fate.
Yet, judging from the ways of men,
they'd find a new way to discriminate,
some other irrationality
besides judging one by one's skin,
instead of by one's character,
would be the new absurdity
to drive the "hate" machinery.
It's sad that I should think this way –
but I still hope for a better day.
That's why I am a dreamer.
And I am not alone; I am sure
there are other dreamers, too!
As I am one, O so can you,
for Ghandi was a dreamer,
and King was a dreamer,
and Christ was a dreamer, too.

II.   A Celebration
of
Life's Four Seasons

When With A Sigh Or Whisper

When with a sigh or whisper
soft and dying snow
surrenders quietly, reluctantly to go,
as if departing, even for snow,
must be the hardest thing to do.

When after twilight breaking,
a bright, sweet-tempered dawn
smiles as it sees the snow move on
after a lengthy sojourn
that buried past hopes in the ground;

When that a fresh fluffed bud
peaks out from its drear prison,
as from a dungeon into light arisen,
and in the air, a sweet sensation breeds
that multiplies and touches where it leads,

then from the spell that winter casts
Earth comes alive again at last,
and fields and hills surrounding
and every creature living
echoes in silence or with singing:

"It's spring!... It's spring!!... It's spring!

What Is Spring

Spring is nature harmonizing,
truth and beauty intertwining,
heaven and earth in chorus singing,
universal love beckoning,
promises richly o'er flowing,
glorious tidings echoing
joy to all mankind.

Spring is nature's way of giving
color to the joy of living,
new hope to the spirit grieving,
blessings to the heart believing,
sweetness to the soul forgiving,
praises to the undeceiving,
love to all mankind.

Spring is nature's way of saying
to the proud life, sometimes straying,
to the contrite heart that's praying,
to the soul that's old and graying,
to the young hearts sprightly playing,
to the lovers love repaying,
"There is hope yet for mankind!"

Spring Rapture

Look around and listen keenly!
Spring excites the atmosphere!
You can savor it freely.
It is throbbing everywhere.
It is rich; drink of it deeply,
with your senses, drink your share.

From the soaring heights of heaven
to the breast of earth below,
all that lie within are laden
with spring's wondrous overflow.

When the world began, the first day
I believe was in the spring,
for to start life's odyssey
there could be no better beginning
than to greet the heart this way
or the soul and bid it sing.

If the world started in winter
there would be no point in spring,
and the spirit would surrender
long before it learned to sing.

Thanks to Heaven for sunshine streaming,
for the blessings of spring rain,
for the joys of new life beaming
that this season brings again!
Everywhere, gay sounds are peeling
Spring's voluptuous refrain:

"Drink, drink gladly! Drink, drink madly!
Drink the rapture I bring you
till your depth is sated fully
and your heart drunk from its brew."

Beauty is in the wide sky, smiling
iridescent poetry;
nature's in the parks inviting
you to share her purity.
Even mute structures surrounding
are alive with harmony.

Lofty skyscrapers, tall standing
give an air of majesty,
of unbounded dreaming, searching
to find immortality!

Nightfall comes with its own blending
like a rapturous serenade.
Its enchantments are revealed in
quite a mystical parade:
starlight gleaming, moonlight streaming
on earth's silhouette cavalcade.

Day has magic, but the violet
touch of night mysteries unfolds;
Earth by daylight, wears her trinkets,
but by night, she wears her soul!

All the bliss there is in living
cannot hold in one small room,
cries for space, demanding, piercing
through the walls of trivial gloom
till the heart, drunk from receiving,
swells to bear these treasures soon.

Spring, it seems, will not allow
her splendors to be shrugged away—
night ends, dawn's new flood of joy
bursts in on our human play.

What is pain 'mid so much pleasure?
Never speak that word again.
What is love if not the treasure
of a soul's boundless domain—
All of our mortal endeavors
flow from it and back again.

O let me taste this vintage sating
every nerve and vein I own;
O, let me drink this wine-inflating
my soul till in it I drown.

To a Songbird

Charmer of dryads! Melodious bird!
What sweet strains you weave high in the trees!
What is the cause of your bliss, wondrous bird?
Can it be that the blossoms and flowers of spring,
the green earth, warm sunshine, and gentle breeze
are what inspire you to sing?

Most marvelous songster in the shape of a bird,
free spirit endowed with a golden art,
what fields and forests lately heard
you thrill the dew-filled morning air?
Your strains are made to melt the heart
and blend with beauty what we hear.

Troubadour of the trees, noble bard among birds,
pouring from the depth of your breast with such ease
unpremeditated songs without words,
what faint heart would not leap for joy
when cascading notes fall out of the trees
in spellbinding melodies you employ?

O happy minstrel, sweet-throated bird,
melt now my heart with your musical stream!
What a loss it would be if this earthly world
knew not, blithe spirit, such bliss as you bring!
Beauty and joy might never have been
if it were that a songbird did not sing.

The Birds of Spring

In spring, you can hear all the little ones
stirring in their nests, crying, *tweet, tweet, tweet*
as their parents return from gathering food
to fill their bellies with enough to eat.

All spring and summer, they grow and grow,
keeping parents busy every day like a ferry,
back and forth with flies, beetles, grubs, worms
and everything good that their stomachs can carry.

Back and forth, miles and miles they travel
in the fields and bushes, no time to tarry.
They must feed their young to grow strong for the journey.
Parents' lives are so tough; no rest for the weary!

By the time summer ends, the chicks are full grown,
their muscles are strong, their wings are well tested.
Yes, they're full grown, well trained to be on their own
while their parents are glad at last to be rested.

And ready to join up with the gathering flock
of their kind getting ready to fly away south!
If you listen, you can hear their chatter and shouts,
"Get into formation, find your places; we're moving out!"

Then you see the most beautiful V-shaped formations
as flock after flock are skyward bound,
until next spring when the travelers return
again to the woodlands, their old stomping ground!

Does this sound familiar? It certainly should!
We are no different, we humans, in many ways.
We raise our young ones and train them well
for the journey of life till the end of our days!

Rue Paul the Fledgling Goose

One day, the fledgling goose, Rue Paul,
full of curiosity and gall
asked his grandpa, the old gray goose,
questions you never should ask a goose!
"Grandpa, grandpa, why do birds fly?
How long do birds live before they die?
And when they die, where do they go?
Where do they go, Grandpa, do you know?"

"My little gosling, you're much too young
to be asking questions so profound!"
"I know, Grandpa, but even so,
tell me the answers, I want to know!"
"First of all, munchkin, all birds must fly!
From very young they must take to the sky
the way their ancestors have always done
to seek food wherever it can be found

and to stay clear of danger all around
from predators who are lurking on the ground.
As seasons change, birds must move on
to climates and pastures that are beyond
the hills and the oceans, and if they
didn't fly, there'd be no birds today!
As for how long before we die,
There are many things that birds of the sky

Have to look out for, one is a hunter's gun!
If one of them doesn't shoot you down,
If you don't, by mistake, fly into a wall
or a building that is standing too tall,
If a speeding car doesn't hit you on the highway,
or an airplane doesn't crush you one day,
If raccoons, foxes, or snakes on the prowl,
or hawks and falcons who like to eat fowl

don't catch you (Hopefully they won't!)
and if diseases don't kill you or pesticides don't,
and hurricanes, floods, and ice storms don't get you
and you manage to survive all these things, I bet you
you might just live to be as old as twenty-three
like an old gray geezer just like me;
and you might die in your sleep if you are lucky,
or plummet from the sky, too old to make the journey!

But don't you worry your head that you won't survive!
Even human beings have problems staying alive!
They die every day, too, from guns, drugs, and wars
that destroy countless lives and inflict countless scars!
And they have epidemics, too, catastrophes, and disease,
so don't think they are immune by being humans, please!
All species are victims to one thing or another;
but I wouldn't change my life for any other!

As for your last question, my answer is this:
If humans can go to a place of perfect bliss
called Heaven when they die, after all they have done
on this earth, being that they are no paragons,
why then, certainly, they must let birds like us in!
The worst we have done is fly around, honk, and swim
and I never heard of a goose that ever did sin!
With no guilty conscience, then, we geese got to get in!

Gardenias

Sweet gardenias, flowers that bloom
against a luscious field of green,
when plucked their fragrant flowers groom
the hair of many a beauty queen.

Their white, pink, and their yellow hues
enrich our gardens and wedding décor,
and as boutonnieres are often used
to adorn bridegrooms, best men, and more.

Gardenias they convey such joy
to whom they are given and are thought much of.
If you're lost for words and feeling coy,
gardenias can express your secret love.

I love gardenias for their sweet perfume,
their exotic nature, their foliage, too,
for the warmth and magic they bring to a room,
but especially because they say, "Be true!"

If You Should See a Lady Fair

(The Message of a Flower)

A lovely lady whom Nature had grown,
gaily her crimson beauty spread
as if for her sunlight had shone
and joyous springtime raised its head.

She smiled as if to say she owned
her fate, and grief to her was unknown.
She seemed a queen upon her throne,
though soon her brief reign would be gone!

I came along and saw her then
and wondered if she only knew
that time would soon announce her end,
and there was nothing she could do!

But she returned a smile to me
as if to say she held the key
to time and immortality
that frowned on my philosophy.

I wondered then if through this flower
Heaven had sent a message of hope
that comes not in great pomp and power
but as a sweet, harmonious note!

Surely, time measures not the worth
of this flower here now, gone tomorrow!
Brief though the time between its birth
and death, what matters anyhow?

Many may live and count their years,
but have no more when all is done
to show for life but grief and tears
and leave no joy when they are gone.

But this, this flower, a life so fleeting,
more than its dues has paid today,
and will continue to make hearts sing
long after it has faded away.

Summer Days Are Over

It's over, it's over, it's over;
days of summer are all gone!
It is now late in October
and the love affair is done!

No more barbecues and picnics,
no more frolicking until dark,
no more street fiestas and ferias,
no more concerts in the park.

Time to put on clothes and cover
all the parts that were laid bare
in the golden days of summer,
for a chill is in the air!

No more wood pushing on park benches
'till the last daylight's displaced;
no more summer barnstorming,
time cannot be reversed.

No more hiking, no more camping
under a deep and starry sky;
no more exploring, woodland trekking,
glorious summer days, goodbye!

It's over, it's over, it's over!
All the crowds have disappeared.
Time to say goodbye to nature
and to friends of yesteryear!

Very soon, leaves will be falling,
and the trees will all be bare;
then, the summer joys and laughter
will be memories to share!

If I Were a Poet

If I were a poet, I couldn't help but show it,
for I'd paint many pictures in rhyme.
I'd rhyme a rainbow, just as you see it,
to last a long, long time.

If I were a poet, you'd certainly know it,
for I'd set down into rhyme
a rose so resplendent that naught could undo it,
not even the passage of time.

If I were a poet, my very next sonnet
would be a Robin's song
whose joy ever fleeting would live, once I've penned it,
after the robin is gone!

If I were a poet, I'd capture the spirit
of an eagle in its flight.
Such splendor!...my verses would always display it
though the eagle had vanished from sight!

If I were a poet, I'd capture a comet
as it went streaking by
over the purple silhouette
of mountains against the sky.

If I were a poet, I'd bring home the sunset
that floods the evening sky;
the warmth of that moment when we reveled in it
would never, never die!

Autumn Leaves

Autumn, autumn, your leaves are falling!
When news comes now, it is to say:
Sadly, another leaf has fallen
from off the Tree of Life today!

There was a time news used to be
about who's dating whom or where
is going to be the next house party,
or what's the latest style to wear.

And nothing would be more newsworthy
than who is getting married to whom,
or, save your best outfit, get ready
for the hottest dance that's coming soon.

And always news about the families,
that everyone was doing fine,
would fill discourse with pleasantries
and make sweeter the fruit of the vine.

Yes, when such good news came already
we were so glad to hear and share,
like who graduated summa cum laude
or who gave birth to twins this year.

Then, all the news began to change
and had a different, sadder tone
so that what once might have seemed strange
now can't be blamed on chance alone.

O Autumn, Autumn, it's so unfair!
Bring me no more sad news today.
The tree of life will be too bare
if all the leaves are gone away!

It Is a Lonely Sight to See

It is a lonely sight to see
naked branches on a tree,
when it was not that long ago
there were so many leaves to show.

Trees all around were thick and green
and sheltered many nests unseen!
Branches stretched far with leaves thereon
all reaching out to kiss the sun!

Now, where did all the green leaves go
and all the friends we used to know?
There were so many long ago
before Autumn and threat of snow!

Most have now fallen to the ground
like leaves of autumn, one by one,
but yet a few cling to the tree,
waiting and wondering patiently.

Too Soon A Rose Must Die

Too soon, a rose must die
and leave no vestige of its charms
to greet the open sky
and deck the autumn scene!

Too soon, chill winter ushers in
and covers with its mantle white
the hills and fields of green
where summer joys had been!

Too soon, the fiddler's tune plays out
and sings no more
what yesterday was all about
when it is gone!

Too soon!...yet swift though time must go,
a heart that lived and loved shall know
't was worth it Love did bloom and grow
if only for an hour.

Spring, Summer, Autumn, Winter

Here's to the memory of spring
when life was mellow, and songs were new!
How we awakened to its calling!
It was the best time that we knew.

In fact, it was the closest ever
that we had come to Eden's shore
when we could run and never tire
and dared winter to reach our door!

Youth's brilliant garden was a-blooming
and happy days had taken root;
the vines were strong, the trees were grooming
and branches readied to bear fruit!

Then came spring's sequel, summertime,
when Nature's children were full-grown;
when seedlings, at last in their prime,
tested their powers until well honed!

Summer, ah summer, mating, parenting time
when Nature's work was at its height!
Seedlings birthed seedlings in their time,
and day was longer than the night!

Gardens were flourishing in the sunlight;
whoever thought of autumn, then?
The earth was good, the future bright,
moving along, time seemed a friend!

But, O, bright summer gave way to autumn,
just as spring gave way to summer, too!
And autumn, fading, passes the baton
to stern winter awaiting its cue!

Blow, blow, you autumn winds,
scatter your leaves once green, now brown!
O fateful autumn that reminds
us spring and summer days are gone!

Maybe you're not to blame, but, O,
you bring sad thoughts as your winds blow,
of friends and loved ones who are no more,
who once shared joys long, long ago!

You hint of cold blasts and winter snow,
O autumn, while your changing hues
show us how hard it is to let go
the joys of youth that we must lose!

Wait, wait, harsh winter, I insist!
Let not your bitter cold chill come!
Compared to you, autumn is bliss,
and does not freeze a lily pond!

O, but a few friends still remain
to face the winter of old age!
How many shall we see again
after life's bitter winter's rage?

The Swan's Song

Within the realm of nature
all species know when it is time
to return again to their maker.
Some may protest or try to flee,
although it will avail them not;
Some go without a sigh or whimper
as death o'er takes their weary lot.
But one greets death magnificently.
I speak about the muted swan
that through its life sings not a note,
yet when the end is close at hand
sends from its bursting lungs so sweet
a parting song or plea to God,
not in protest but exultation,
as if to say, "Here I am, Lord,
your prodigal child returning home,"
and, folding its wings, closes its eyes,
then slumps, lifeless, to earth and dies.

A Winter Sonnet

Autumn sends out its sweeping breath, announcing,
"Now put away your summer things and pleasures!"
Creatures are busy storing away their treasures
for needy days, knowing that winter's coming!
And when the dreadful cold on earth is pouncing
they know, while sleeping, winter's drastic measures
though dreadful pass, and soon glorious new pleasures
will rise again and be theirs in the spring.

So why are we afraid of winter's coming
and pine that summer days for us are gone?
It is as natural as the swallows leaving,
and there may yet be a glorious new beginning
after the blistering winter's course is done!
It must follow, if winter then comes spring!

III. LOVE

Courting

There are things you see in nature
that inspire and amaze,
such as how birds choose a partner
and their fascinating ways.

For example, take a sparrow
who works hard to build a house,
then stands outside, poor fellow,
trying his best to get a spouse!

He calls out to female sparrows,
"Come and see my pretty house!"
If one female likes it, kudos,
he has found himself a spouse.

The king bird of paradise, now he
is one impressive sight, bar none!
Tail quivering, chest fluffed up, deftly
he swings like a swinging pendulum.

I don't know what the female thinks,
but never has she seen before
such brilliant acrobatic feats
and falls for it, you can be sure.

But if you think the king is something,
you haven't seen anything until
you've seen the red-cap manikin
put on a floorshow that could kill!

He flies off, returns, wings flapping
and swoops down on a branch nearby,
then does the greatest moonwalking
to catch a moonstruck female's eye;

And she, curious and fascinated,
comes closer and closer to see.
Then she cannot leave; she's checkmated,
and the two start a family.

Of course, we know how the robin sings
and the female answers if she likes his tune.
Winged Caruso stretches his vocal strings
and before you know it, he has a bride in June!

Now, the African lovebirds of the parrot family,
they kiss, pass food from beak to beak,
engage in foreplay and then get busy.
They are serious, too, and marry for keeps.

They are not the only ones that take
the marriage vows and bonding to heart;
the Canadian goose makes a pact with its mate,
and the trumpeter swan, "Till death do us part!"

And there are many more species, I suppose,
that bond together for a very long time,
while, on the other hand, there are those
who are just looking to have a good time?

They pair just for sex and then disappear,
like the sage grouse, sandpiper, and hummingbird;
but they're not the most promiscuous, for there
are the swallow and the Australian wren—take my word.

Birds also practice polygamy
like the red-winged blackbird and the meadowlark,
and some even go in for polyandry
like the phalarope who makes males do housework.

She runs around multiple mating!
She leaves behind for each of her mates
the jobs of incubating and housekeeping
while she goes off on secret dates!

Birds are more amazing than I can say,
and I wonder which species, bird or man,
is better at courting! Anyway,
birds are more colorful by nature's plan.

On Hearing Two Lovebirds In The Woods

Sing! Sing your hearts out, songbirds, sing!
Your gift is song, your stage is spring!
Up from the fountains in your breasts
pour out your songs and let the wind,
that famous courier of swiftness,
send out its message, echoing

to all the earth awakening
into a dream from dreaming!
O boldly let your rich pipes play
and yield charms unabating;
a cozy nest not far away
in paradise is waiting!

Sing, tune-swept hearts! O creatures blessed,
for paradise is a noble quest!
All nature and I, too, witness
your vows and your sweet trilling!
Soon, you shall realize the bliss
that comes from love fulfilling!

Pray, may your warblings ever flow.
'Till all the world with gladness glow
from such enchantment -- your duet
teaches a sad heart how to sing,
and shows a soul how to forget
the scars that often to life cling!

A Painted Lady

One bright and sunny afternoon, the air
was filled with fragrances of perfume everywhere!
The streets were paved in sun-drenched sheets, and on
the joy-swept sidewalks light steps came along:
a painted lady from whom radiance shone,
with jewels in her hair that sparkled in the sun,
was walking in that summer air stately and sure,
was walking, greeting all with smiles and with allure!
The earth appeared to rise to meet her shifting feet;
her swerving hips and shoulders moved in rhythmic beat
and yielded to the pleasing whole
their share of splendor to behold!
Upon the lawn, the grass blades bowed their heads and sighed,
"She walks! She walks in painted beauty magnified!"
I gave my heart away that sunny day;
but when the paint and glitter wore away,
I longed for simple virtue, modest clay,
and not a painted lady on display.

Dorothy

O Dorothy, sweet Dorothy,
you look so very fine,
all chocolate brown and sugary,
tell me that you'll be mine!

O John Daly, O John Daly,
although I must confess
you have a very sweet tongue, really
I cannot tell you yes.

O Dorothy, sweet Dorothy
with eyes of amber hue,
your lips look soft and savory,
they say I must have you.

O John Daly, O John Daly,
my mother told me one thing:
Let no sweet-talking Dandy
win me without a ring.

O Dorothy, sweet Dorothy,
you put me through a lot;
I have a chariot with me,
but a ring I haven't got.

O John Daly, O John Daly,
then trade your chariot in;
I wish to see only
a golden wedding ring!

O Dorothy, sweet Dorothy,
you're asking for a lot,
but first, it's only fair for me
to sample what you've got.

O John Daly, O John Daly,
I'm no cook shop or market
where you can sample freely—
What you see is what you get!

So Dorothy kept her virtue
for the right man to come along,
and told John Daly what he could do
with his sweet-talking tongue.

But slick John Daly knew that he
could never win them all.
"The odds," he said, "are still with me.
It takes just one to fall!"

When I Was Young

When I was young and passing seventeen,
I was quite shy and also very green!
I met a girl whose name was "Dancing Doreen;"
Since she taught me, a dancer I have been.

When I was young and tried to be a dandy,
I met a girl I called, "O my, Miss Mandy!"
She was so fine she was like sugar candy,
and I was thrilled to be her Handy Dandy!

When I was young and I was slightly handsome,
I courted quite a few fine, lovely lassies!
I met a girl whose name was Cherry Blossom,
and she was so much sweeter than molasses!

When I was young and I was somewhat carefree,
I met a girl whose name was Caroline!
I showed her things, the things she showed to me
I cannot say, but they were so divine!

When I was young, and I was not too choosy,
I met a girl whose name was "Dizzy Suzie."
She took me for a ride, it was a doozie!
She left me breathless and a little woozy!

When I was young while visiting Delancey,
I found the place was not too very fancy!
I met a girl there by the name of Nancy,
who made me change my mind about Delancey!

When I was young while walking through the tulips,
I stopped awhile to admire their regalia;
I took one home, but soon, her nagging lips
made me sick of tulipomania!

When I was young and I was very strong,
I met a girl I called "Hard Time Yvonne!"
I never slaved so hard or tried so long
to win a prize before from anyone!

When I was young, I thought I found true bliss,
I met a girl I called "pro forma" Lorna!
She was a beauty I could not resist;
Later, we parted, O but that "pro forma!"

But I have no regrets at all today,
I loved them all, and they were good to me!
Though we have parted, this much I will say,
we drank the honey…and now must let it be!

Bird Of Paradise

Bird of paradise, joy of life,
I knew the day would have to come
when you would fly away from me
and find yourself another song!

Though I had given you all I could,
I could not give you your desire--
your yearning for new pastures green,
your craving for youth's fleeting fire!

I gave to you a seasoned love,
'twas warm enough to melt the snow
and strong enough to hold back tides,
even as youthful fires burn low;

but you, instead, chose greener fields
and open skies for your domain!
Your restless wings, yearning to fly,
could not within my nest remain!

Now I, earthbound, who loved you so,
must watch you fly away from me!
In spite of all the joy we shared,
In spite of all, I set you free!

O bird of paradise, fly away;
your wings were always meant to fly!
My nest is only made of clay
and cannot match the boundless sky.

Summer Sunshine, Summer Rain

Summer sunshine, summer rain
descending on a summer plain!
Summer smiles and summer tears,
memories lasting through the years--
O how very close we came
and never came close again!

Summer fields and gardens green,
raindrops cooling petals seen
in a rapturous summer scene!
It was here where we once met
in a place that time has set
and the heart cannot forget!

Summer winds and summer rain
beating on a window pane,
pouring out an old refrain:--
'Two hearts joined together when
they stayed here awhile, and then
never passed this way again!'

Summer joys and summer pain,
through the mist and through the rain!
O so many summers came,
seasons rolled around again;
but we'll never see the same
summer sunshine, summer rain!

Intimate Expressions To A Past Loved One

Though you are gone, I shall remember
the way you were dressed,
the cap that you bore,
the style of your hair,
the sweater you wore,
the beads 'round your neck,
your close-fitting slacks
and your smart leather boots!

Though you are gone, I shall remember
the way you said, "Hello," and I said, "Hye,"
the way that the chemistry started to flow
with a kiss upon greeting that promised much more!
I shall remember our sipping some wine
which you liked, and I said I shall always provide;
I'll remember your comment about the moon,
"It must be a U.F.O.," you said,
as it vanished for a moment out of view,
and I laughed and replied, "How could that be?
Your imagination fascinates me!"

Though you are gone, I shall remember
the touch of your cheeks against my face,
the feel of my hands caressing your skin,
the taste of your lips opening for my own,
the fire of your tongue searching to find mine,
the throbbing of our breasts, sigh after sigh,
the ecstacy thrilling through our beings
while we were locked in sweet embrace,
and, oh, the longing for time to stand still
when it seemed that our hearts were about to burst
and we wanted them to, rather than subside!

Though you are gone, I shall remember
the scent of your hair, your sweet perfume,
the glow in your eyes, the flush of your cheeks,
the hating to go when we wanted to stay,
the clasping again to renew our embrace
even while we were parting, for our hearts would not go
as our lips found each other again and again,
and the words kept repeating from your lips and mine,
"I love you... I love you... I love you so...!"

Though the dance is now over, and what's done is done,
though you've gone away, and I am alone
in the dimness of life's twilight zone,
though the days grow short and the nights are long,
on a cold winter's night, with the thermostat set right,
and a sip of sweet wine to heighten memory,
I shall remember the things that used to be,
as it was in the days gone by for you and me,
and I'll hold you again in my arms once again,
and I'll kiss you again… and again… and again…!

The Coin

He keeps it safe within his wallet
inside a secret compartment
and never takes it out except
sometimes, when sad and spent

And he's alone, no one watching!
He'd reach into his back pocket,
dreading it could be missing,
thinking he might have dropped it

The last time he had looked at it!
Then reassured, fortunately,
his fears were quelled when he felt it
and clutched it, O, so tenderly!

If only that coin could tell its story
how, from all the coins in all the land
It was the one by destiny
that ended up in Celia's hand!

In her hand, one touch and that nickel
was never evermore the same!
She gave it to him when they were little
to hold, to keep it in their name.

It was a coin, it was a dream,
a hope of two hearts long ago;
It was a coin two hearts had deemed
was their down payment for tomorrow.

"When we have saved enough," she said,
"we'll buy a castle for love to grow!"
It sounded real, so real, granted;
but what do little children know?

Not long after that, her family
had packed, and they all left the town;
then months and years weighed heavily
even on one who was so young.

He tried his best to forget her
and the dream that one day they would join;
yet it was strange he couldn't surrender
or spend that precious five-cent coin!

Growing up, he looked for her, not knowing
that she had gone to a foreign land;
and she, in turn, tried writing him
which was an unsuccessful plan!

One day, he, too, reached that land –
It must have been the coin of fate
that worked its magic and played a hand
to lead him there, but, O, too late!

He mentioned her name to a friend
who knew her, and she told him of
the story of Celia's sad end!
How she had sought to find new love

In a strange land with a stranger!
It wasn't the love of long ago,
still, she tried to make it work for her.
Alas, it brought disaster, though!

How could she know death was the stranger
in that far-off distant land?
Her heart was once pledged to another
but fate dealt her a different hand.

"If you would find your Celia now,
she is lying in the cemetery.
She's gone!" Life never is, somehow,
the way children wish it could be.

The friend was sad; he, even more so,
for dearest Celia, whom he once knew.
How ties of childhood will not let go
of love so innocent that once rang true!

He held the coin, fought back the tears,
then placed it in his wallet and
was glad he kept it all these years—
the coin that once touched Celia's hand!

So The Beauty of Her Face

Like a rosebud plucked too soon
ere it formed into a rose;
like a book just when it opened
Fate stepped in and had it closed;

like a promise of delight
that never saw the light of day;
like a hope that burned too bright
ere the light was taken away –

so the beauty of her face
and her heart that I remember.
They shall never be erased
from my memory forever!

Eternal Love

(Is love a more powerful force than death? This poem is dedicated to two young people who lived and loved and died for love. Shakeem and Kumarie could not live without each other, and so when Shakeem was tragically murdered, Kumarie committed suicide so that in death, they would be together. Although they died tragic deaths, we should not be
sad for them, for they died with the certainty that their love
would live forever.)

Shakeem, Shakeem,
true lover of mine,
sweet is your love today;
but will you love me when I'm
feeble, old, and gray?

Kumarie, Kumarie,
when we're old and gray
love will be like wine sublime;
age shall make harshness melt away
and sweeten us more with time.

Shakeem, Shakeem,
sweet is your love, I know;
but when I shake and bend,
beloved, even so,
how will you love me then?

O Kumarie, dear Kumarie,
know this: my heart shall see
you then the same as now,
though countless years may flee
and we are old and bowed.

O Shakeem, sweet is your vow,
but though you love me now,
all things, I fear, must end;
and when I'm dead and gone,
how will you love me then?

O dearest Kumarie,
our love shall never die!
There is a place you'll see,
a place for you and me,
etched in eternity

where I shall love you still;
and though we're changed, we will
be timeless as the skies;
and time will not the cheater be
however swift it flies!

O Shakeem, sweet lover true,
how shall I know 'tis you
if we are changed? Tell me
Shakeem, how it shall be,
how you shall still love me!

O Kumarie, O Kumarie,
whom I dearly adore,
ten thousand years or more
I'll still love you:
If you're a bird, I'll still be true,
I'll be the wind beneath you
that lifts you as you soar
above the seas from shore to shore.

O Shakeem, Shakeem,
sweet lover of mine,
your words are so sublime,
your pledges are so sweet,
With them I am complete!
Now tell me one more time,
then seal your heart with mine.

O Kumarie, O Kumarie,
hear now this solemn vow:
Ten thousand years from now
If you're an angel, I'll be the sunshine
that warms your face divine;

If you're a flower
I'll worship at your vine
and be charmed every hour.
If I'm a bee, you'll be my honey;
If I'm a sunflower, you'll be my sun;
If I'm a songbird, you'll be my song;
If I'm an oyster, you'll be my pearl!
You'll be my rainbow in my world,
my treasure and my happiness
as you are now, and I'll be blessed
ten times ten thousand times, you'll see.
And though eons may flee,
whatever else may be,
when you shall ask of me,
Do you still love me now?"
Just like a star, O Kumarie,
the brightest in the skies,
you'll sparkle in my eyes
and I'll be answering still,
"Yes, yes, my love, and always will
for all eternity!"

Epilogue:

I believe that on some dark nights
If you look up to the sky and see
two bright stars twinkling very close
together in the heavens; or on
a clear summer day if you should see
two sunflowers kissing in the sun,
or two lovebirds soaring sublimely in
the skies above, and you are moved,
be not surprised; it is Shakeem
and Kumarie, that you see,
expressing true love for each other,
inseparably forever and forever.

A Pearl of Great Value

Once in the carefree days of yore
when I was filled with youthful vigor,
untarnished, heart still young and pure,
I came upon a great, great treasure.

It was a priceless pearl I had never
seen before, whose value grew greater
the more I pondered how I could ever
attain it with all my life's endeavors.

Then the treasure spoke; it had eyes and lips
and a face so beautiful I could not resist.
I prayed, "Make her mine, O Holiness,
in exchange for all in this world I possess!"

I sought that treasure that seemed so divine
and soon, all the stars above were aligned;
and just when it seemed, she was almost mine,
when our two hearts were about to entwine,

a dark cloud intervened, and when it dispersed,
the darkness had shifted my universe.
I lost that treasure, and I've searched in vain
but I never could find that treasure again.

In my sadness, though, an angel said to me:
"Do not despair finding your treasure again;
sometimes treasures lost on earth mysteriously
are discovered again somewhere in Heaven."

Dedicated to all who have lost an earthly treasure.

Love is Like a Flower

Graceful is a flower
growing on a vine,
made from sun and shower
and a seed combined.
Fair and frail and fragrant
fresh and rich and rare,
king and lowly vagrant
have found treasures there.

Love is like a flower
growing on life's vine,
made from tears and laughter
and a pledge combined.
It grows ever sacred
when it shall endure;
they have been rewarded
who have found love's shore.

The Rose Garden

There is a garden of roses
sweeter than blooms of May,
ever the warmth it exposes
transcends the fetters of clay.

Fashioned, this garden of roses,
with consummate care and art,
throughout the years, it discloses
beauty that comes from the heart!

When you need flowers around you
to brighten the place where you stay,
come to that garden grown for you
and pick out a lovely bouquet!

There are roses of understanding,
roses of passion true,
roses of kindness attending
all to the love of you!

There are roses of friendship enduring,
roses of hope ever new,
roses of trust never failing,
all for the love of you!

Flowers that bloom in the springtime
wither and soon must decay;
but those that grow in love's sunshine
will never fade away!

Smitten by a Rose

I was once smitten by a rose
when visiting in a southern land.
I do not know how the heart knows
what the mind cannot understand—
How, in a fleeting moment, one spark
could fly across a crowded room
from one sweet rose to ignite my heart.
In God's garden of flowers that bloom,
never had I seen a flower with such grace
as if an angel from Heaven came down
and settled in a human face.

In God's garden of flowers that bloom
this lovely rose so melted my heart!
She moved blithely across the room
and like an arrow that found its mark
said to me softly, "Hurry back soon,
I hope you make this land your home!"
Then, I felt saddened to have to depart
and planted a kiss on her cheek.
She seemed a child in matters of the heart --
so sweet and innocent with eyes that speak!

I hadn't the courage or will to say
what sadly I had already known --
even while her eyes melted my heart away --
that when I from that land had flown
I would not see her face again,
for she was to another wed
and our flight of fancy had to end
with that sad goodbye instead!
O poor dark eyes, you can't help but live
like a flower so bright to be admired,
knowing your heart is not free to give
no matter how much it may be desired.

I Remember April

I remember April,
sweet, nostalgic April,
with new grass at her feet,
the wind dancing in her hair,
her cheerful ways to greet,
her smiling face so fair,
her pretty skirts so neat
'gainst green lawns everywhere.

I remember April
when apple blossoms, sweet
their spring ritual enact,
and plants are not discreet
attracting birds and bees to extract,
like airborne winged dragoons,
their first spring sips of sweetness
from pollen-laden blooms!

I remember April,
warm and tender April,
torrential tears and all,
nourishing and enriching
wherever they might fall,
and her sweet breath, caressing
my cheeks to make me feel
so glad that I am living.

Yes, I remember April
calling, calling me:
"There's so much love to give!
O come now and be merry,
this is the time to live!
See how I make birds sing!
See how I color things,
and all the joy I bring!"

Yes, I remember when
true love was first in bloom,
and fresh buds were awakened
to hear its happy tune!
I remember, I remember,
how could I ever forget?
Love sealed April forever
as the best time yet!

Lament for a Lost Love

O speak no more to me of love,
that ever veiled, illusive phantom
that came to me from Heaven above
long, long ago when I was young.
Now time grows late, and I grow weary
left with a sad and broken song.
What if… O haunting memory…
What if we had not said goodbye
and could return in time once more
to where your beauty first caught my eye!
I remember walking through a door
and in a moment, in one sigh
of bliss, our hearts met and, behold,
a love awakened that said to me:
"Would that this were John Keats' Ode
On a Grecian Urn, time would take hold
of her beauty as she smiles at me
and freeze it in eternity…
and I would share true love with her
forever in time's work of art!"
O better that than losing her,
better that by far than a broken heart
or a promise that vanished in an hour!
O love that showed your face to me
and blossomed in my heart a flower
in the days of my youth's purity,
had we not met, perhaps 't were better
than to have known how great a loss,
how sad parting from you would be
and how unbearable the cost;
but we did meet, and I can't forget you.
I think of you each day and hour
and long once more to see your face --

so that before the dreaded winter
removes all doubt --- it would be said:
"They met and wrote their final chapter,
the last for which the first was made."
Yet even if the bleakest future
must now be, know that we came close,
close as a heartbeat and did not capture
what should have been, Heaven only knows,
had some untimely misadventure
not brought true love to its close.
O rule of life, too cruel, I fear,
that gives one chance for perfect bliss!
I grieved when I saw you disappear
into the whirlwind and the mist.

I Had Thought to Love was Best

I had thought to love was best…
and even if love's burning quest
should lead me to the end of the earth
with two choices to crown my search:
Either live a long life and know not love,
or live one moment with boundless love,
I would choose love.

I had thought to love was best…
and even if while on love's quest,
were I forbidden in all the land
to love you and to hold your hand,
though death be my fate or reward yet,
so let it be; I would not regret
that I chose love.

I had thought it best to love…
and not to speak ill about love
no matter how much anger riles me,
no matter how grave deeds defile me,
for there's no wrong, and there's no slight
too great that love cannot make right,
therefore, I love.

I had thought to love was best…
and even if put to the test
to see if love is really blind,
I would fail that test each time;
for I shall find no fault in you,
no matter what they say or do…
because of love.

I had thought it best to love...
and never doubt the power of love
to transform darkness into light,
and change sadness to sweet delight;
So, from all doubts and mistrust turning,
with all my heart and being yearning,
I choose to love.

I had thought to love was best,
that, somehow, love could be kept
in a true, inviolate state,
even if that would dictate
freezing it in time to stay
forever fresh as yesterday.
So, be then, love...

that the greatest bliss shall be
love froze in time for you and me,
and you'll be beautiful forever,
and I'll forever worship you,
and stars shall fade before we do,
and eternity will prove how true
it is to love.

The Mystery of Love

When we were young, and love was new
you asked me how I knew I loved you.
I answered true and said to you,
"Just as I knew there is Heaven, too,
and just as I knew that flowers knew
when they opened their eyes and looked into
the wonder of sunlight shining through
that they loved the sun…that's how I knew."

You asked again, "How could you know
you loved me so?" I said, "Let's go
and ask God for He put the glow
and magic in you; then He must know
when He made you, what that would do
to my poor heart on seeing your glow.
Seeing you, I knew the way to go
to Paradise… that's all I know."

"How could you know that you loved me?"
you cried. I said, "If words alone
sufficed, my lips would set them free
and the mystery would be made known;
but it seems that words and reasoning
alone cannot explain God's wisdom --
How we can know without knowing
is a mystery until kingdom come.

Believe me, I knew that I loved you
even before words came to me;
every cell and fiber in me knew
to love you was my destiny."
You turned to me and whispered low:
"I believe you now; my heart says so!"
And then you gave your heart to me
and thus was solved love's mystery.

IV.   TRAVELLING
IN
DISTANT LANDS

The Dungeons of Cape Coast Castle

Ghana, West Africa

The ocean roars, the waves rush in
with heavy sighs and mighty groans
like the sounds of a million sorrows gushing!
They rush and die in effusive moans

against the rocks on Cape Coast shore.
Since souls first suffered, I am sure
that all oceans that ever roared
have washed their tears on mankind's shore.

Today, in the dungeons underground,
I walked in Hell where countless bled,
stifled in darkness and stench profound.
O walls, still reeking of the dead!

I felt in darkness spirits around me,
millions rising up from the dust,
pleading woefully from eternity,
"Remember us! Remember us!"

I think of the cruelty and horror, and I
know that I'll forever hear those cries,
millions of God's children condemned to die
in dungeons like these, where the horror never dies.

And even if some did survive
these horrors for the sister dungeons
in the bellies of slave ships, it was to live
in another hell! O the lucky ones

they perished quickly who wished for death,
whose souls despaired, whose spirits, bereft
of any hope, gave up their breath
in the dungeons or in the ocean's depth.

The ocean pummels against the shores
as its rhythmic salvos lash and spray.
All through the night and day, she roars;
maybe she frees herself that way.

She willingly had no part in it,
although her depths were certainly used
as a graveyard for crimes she did not commit,
but was forced to join in with the accused.

As I lay on my pillow that night alone,
I heard the ocean and the waves rush in
like the sound of a million gasps and groans
and a million last breaths of the dying…dying…

In manmade dungeons, dungeons of Hell!
I do not wonder that the ocean roars
and moans till nothing seems to quell
It's violent lashing against the shores!

O ocean wail, O groan, and moan,
for in your bosom rests countless bones
that once were chained inside a dungeon,
then tossed into a sea of oblivion.

Wail, ocean, wail against the shore,
wail, souls that in your billows roar,
wail, wail forevermore,
till mankind rights its wrongs of yore.

Horemakhet (or the Great Sphinx of Egypt)

O grand colossus carved in stone
four thousand five hundred years ago,
how many empires have come and gone,
and still, your presence marvels so!

O mighty guardian of the dead,
crouched on this sandy desert floor,
shaped like a lion with a king's head,
rising six stories high or more

and stretching a city block in length,
you've withstood man, nature, and time
and are a symbol of great strength,
foreboding evils yet undefined.

O that you even exist somehow
to gaze transfixed, timeless, and true,
is wonder enough. I would by now
be dust of dust like them who carved you.

Grand in your loneliness, you stand
in mystery and veiled solemnity,
a fitting testament to ancient man
for all eternity.

The Great Pyramid of Giza

O ancient pyramid standing tall
above the sandy desert floor,
oldest of seven wonders, yet all
but you have vanished and are no more.
For almost four millennia now
you've left the ancient world behind;
and though your purpose may be known,
what still remains a mystery
is how they built you stone upon stone
with almost perfect symmetry,
a square base, six football fields long
measuring three thousand feet around,
and a height fifty-seven stories high.
Once you were the tallest structure known,
trying your best to touch the sky.

You are the largest, oldest one
of all the pyramids that can be traced.
It took millions of blocks of stone
cut perfectly and precisely placed,
weighing two and a half tons each one,
to build you, and, with tools back then,
twenty years till the job was done—
and not by slaves but gifted workmen
who took pride in their craft and skill,
perhaps tens of thousands of them,
who built towns near the site to fulfill
their daily lives, like towns today
built near construction sites and factories,
where management, wisely, in the same way
help house workers and their families.
Although that era was much different,
they knew healthy workers built a better monument.

The craftsmen who served, when it was done,
must have felt proud, every last one,
to have had a hand in its construction,
and gained from it honor and distinction.

What we see today is a wondrous sight,
but when first built, each layer was packed
with casing stones of polished white,
making the sides more smooth and flat,
and at the very top, it was crowned
with a capstone that was sheathed in gold
that glittered in the desert sun.
O, what a sight that was to behold!
For centuries, it was left alone;
but time, nature, and man took their toll
and the casings are gone, so the sheath and capstone.

Now, no more pyramids are built to serve
as tombs for the afterlife in store;
and no ointments or embalming can preserve
the flesh for the spirit to occupy once more.
The ancients believed this, which inspired them to plan;
and because of their belief, look what we obtained.
Look at the monuments to the spirit of man,
the treasures, knowledge from the past we have gained.
Such a remarkable achievement perhaps will stand
till the end of time in memory of ancient man.

On the Great Wall of Badaling

While standing on the Great Wall of China,
high up in the region of Badaling,
along with the crowd of people with cameras,
while no one else was noticing,
the ghosts of my ancestors were standing with me
to see this ancient wonder and were smiling.
"We have the great pyramids," they said to me;
"They have the Great Wall above Beijing."
Yes, the Great Spirit gave them a wondrous thing,
a four thousand-mile wall atop mountain peaks
across northern borders, a magnificent feat
built by the dynasties of Qin, Sul, Han, Jin, Ming
and maintained over two thousand years between
the fifth century BC and the sixteenth AD,
built at first with stone, wood, and earth only,
then later with bricks in the Ming Dynasty,
that made it so very strong and sturdy.
Imagine the lives it took to build,
and to drag those materials so far uphill?"
I saw no graves, and yet I knew,
mixed in the earth, stones, bricks, mortar, too,
countless bodies were buried there.
There's a price for all great feats; that's so clear.
I tried to climb to the highest tower,
tower eight; as with the pyramids, however,
I failed to do so; besides, it was such
a treacherous climb. It didn't bother me much,
for even when I could climb no further,
such a view greeted my sight as no other!
It looked as if a great serpentine dragon
went meandering in the distance upon
the vast and perilous mountain ranges,
curving and rising as the mountain changes.

My soul reached out to those who built it,
who stretched the human will and spirit
to build such a thing for all humanity
to see and to last 'till eternity—
and all they had was human labor
and ancient tools and time. It was for
their self-defense, they built this wall,
that I am told, and for it all,
to fend off mankind against mankind
so many lives were lost! I find
it a sad necessity in the end:
That men must protect themselves from men.

Sometimes I think at night the ghosts
of all those men whose lives were lost
building it and whose bones are dust,
mingled with earth and bricks beneath us,
come out and walk along these walls,
though not to admire it as if it was all
such a great piece of work for which to die;
but to gaze on it and to wonder, why?

The Terra-Cotta Warriors of Xian, China

So lifelike, yet made out of clay,
they seem alert, armed to the ready
as if waiting in full battle array
to take the field and engage the enemy
for their emperor Qin Shihuang;
the Terra-Cotta Warriors stand
with horses and chariots, swords, and spears.
They have been waiting thousands of years,
and would be still in their lifeless stance
in the afterlife, if not by chance
farmers of Xian didn't happen to drill
in search of water for their field
in March of nineteen-seventy-four
and stumbled onto much, much more.
because of them, the civilized world
uncovered Qin Shihuang's underworld,
for no one was left alive back then
to tell the secret of Emperor Qin,
that thousands of terra-cotta men
were waiting to someday march again.
Who knows, at least for Qin Shihuang
he died believing he would take command
of his army. That, to him, was real,
though the world can believe whatever it will,
that a legend is no more than a legend,
and dead men can not rise to fight again.

This archeological discovery
has been excavated, though not entirely,
and a museum is built above and around it.
It is a favorite sight to see
whenever you are in Xian City.
Millions of tourists from everywhere
come here to see it every year.
Thank you, Emperor Qin, thank you again;
and thank you, terra-cotta men.

The Silkworm

Suzhou, China

Digressing here from my tour experience,
sometimes I find it a bit expedient
to site some uneventful thing
that changes forever the world we live in.
For instance, how they came to discover
the world's most luxurious natural fiber.
I can't resist telling this little story
that is part of the human anthology:

In two-thousand-forty-six BC,
Lei-Tzu, wife of Emperor Huang Di,
was sitting under a mulberry tree
resting and drinking a hot cup of tea,
when suddenly a cocoon fell from the tree
into her cup and was soaked thoroughly.
It unwounded into a delicate filament
that looked so thin and iridescent.
To her amazement, by twisting together
many fibers that were soaked in the hot water
she had enough soft threads for her spindle
to wind into yarn, then with hands so gentle
she wove them into a ceremonial robe
for the emperor, who, so pleased with the robe,
helped her develop the first silk factory.
Henceforth, Lei-Tzu, for her discovery
was called the Goddess of Silk Making.
A story like this is fascinating,
somehow, it reminds me of Isaac Newton.
There might never have been a law of gravitation
if an apple did not fall on Newton's head.
Anyway, in both cases, credit nature instead.

Returning to the tour in Jiangsu
Province, we came to the city of Suzhou
with its classical gardens and beautiful scenery,
and we visited its famous silk factory
to see how silk is made from the worm
that gives its life so as to adorn
many ladies of distinction who have worn
the finest threads that came from a cocoon.

The worms never know why they're being fattened so
in mulberry heaven, and they'll never know,
as they wrap themselves in silken pouches
within their cocoons in dreamlike crouches
with hopes of becoming a butterfly
to flit about in the summer sky.
They spin their cocoons of silken threads
around themselves and lie in their beds,
forming a chrysalis that is their tomb
and the prize that will occupy many a loom.
Hundreds of thousands of them each day
it takes to make garments on display.
One hundred eleven cocoons make a man's tie;
six hundred thirty, a woman's blouse to please the eye.

In a steaming hot cauldron, the worm dies, and the clean
threads are attached to a spinning machine
that stretches and combines them in a single strand,
each strand unbreakable, and one cocoon can
yield three thousand six hundred feet of thread,
and the strands are combined several times ahead
to make them thicker before they are dyed
by being soaked in boiling dye, turning each side
for an hour to ensure every part absorbs the dye
before they are taken out and set to dry.
When dried, they are rolled onto spools like magic
for the weavers to weave into the finest fabric.

But the worms, the worms, they will never fly,
yet there's one consolation I cannot deny:
instead of a butterfly that will vanish and soon be gone,
they are transformed into a beautiful dress or gown
that for years will adorn my lady's shapely form—
O, it's not so bad after all, being a silkworm.

The Jade Factory in Beijing

Jade has always been fascinating to me;
there is something about it, a certain quality,
In fact, when I see a statue made of jade,
especially one that is masterfully made,
If I stare at it long enough, I am prone
to be touched in spirit—such an ethereal stone.
While in China, we visited a factory in Beijing
on the way to the Great Wall in Badaling.
In the showroom, there were all these statues to see
displayed everywhere majestically.
I saw a herd of horses in dark jade,
a colorful tree, a giant ship well made,
a giant Buddha, a pair of dragons, an eagle in flight,
and they were in all colors as well they might,
for jade comes in many colors, my favorite, green,
and a flower tree was the most beautiful I had seen.
When I asked what was the biggest statue made
out of jade and how much it was weighed,
I was told the one in Xiuyan, which is named
"Beautiful Landscape on a Cliff," has that claim.
It stands ten feet in height by eight feet wide
and weighs eleven tons; my credulity was tried;
but there's more, "The Nine Dragons Fountain," for instance,
in Lushan weighs ten tons, and I hesitated to chance
asking the prices for these enormous carvings,
so I slipped away to look at rings and earrings.
By the way, I was told that the ship I saw
cost a million dollars, and it filled me with awe.

I had wondered where jade comes from, not being erudite,
and learned jade is a hard stone of nephrite or jadeite,
two of the hardest substances for tools to bite,
harder in fact than quartz or granite.
Chinese Durhan jade is the earliest that was mined
as early as six thousand BC, and at one time
Jade had a status value more than gold
and silver in China, so I've been told.

Today jade is found in many parts, not China alone,
though China was the first and most famous to mine the stone;
but even with today's modern equipment jade mining is hard.
Jade is dug out of massive boulders that seem to guard
it with jealous resistance from the miners' grasp.
Drilling with diamond-tipped drills is the first task,
then using hydraulic spreaders inserted in cleavages marked
they break open the boulders, but that's the easy part.
The jade is sometimes forty tons or more
and is the toughest stone for man to bore
or lift or cut, yet, that must be done,
by as slow and difficult a process as they come,
with diesel-operated, water-cooled diamond saws
that split the jade with its diamond-tipped jaws
into manageable ten-ton chunks of jade
and the tools must be kept water-cooled all day
or they'll break throwing thousands of dollars away.
That is why I give the Chinese credit for long ago
they didn't have modern tools, but then we know
how in ancient times what the Egyptians could do
even though they didn't have any modern tools, too.
I marvel at what they do with jade, and their love for the stone
and its value and spiritual significance alone.

The Olgas and Ayers Rock (Uluru) Of Central Australia

From the time we landed at Ayers Rock,
and I saw that the land there was not
green pastures, but arid desert land
with emu bushes, shrubs, and sand
and kangaroo paws and desert peas,
sandalwood, low blue bush, and ghost gum trees,
I wondered what creatures besides tourists
would venture out here in this wilderness.
By noon our private coach reached the resort,
a man-made oasis built in the desert
with green grass, healthy shrubs and thriving plants
co-existing with the desert, growing as transplants
from some pastureland and now sustained
so long as the oasis can be maintained.
For a treat, after checking in and settling down,
and the daylight was still not yet all gone,
we drove to the Olgas and Uluru in the sand
to see the sun set on the outback land,
and witness color changes wrought by the setting sun.
Such a gorgeous experience, we shared it with champagne
as we saw the sun die o'er the majestic desert plain.
Next morning we were off at five, while still dark,
to a rendezvous place in the desert park,
where breakfast was spread on tables in the sand,
and hot and cold drinks to make it grand,
as we waited to see the miraculous sun rising,
lighting up the Olgas and Ayers rock, revealing
their bright earth red colors in the distance,
standing high above ground, which gave their countenance
a mysterious aura, as though they were aware
they were the heroes in a drama taking place there.
The spectacle lasted about ten minutes or a little more,
and we marveled at nature's magnificence on the desert floor.
At a mile-away distance we seemed so close,
only when we approached nearer, we saw how grandiose
Ayers Rock is, a mile high, you could make the case.
It would take many miles to circle her base.
Needless to say, no one dared to climb her;
and we left impressed by the work of Nature.

The Aborigines Of Australia

Before I came here I knew so little
about this land, about its people,
the Aborigines who are dark like me.
It wouldn't surprise me if our ancestry
bore a common strain from across the oceans.
They were the first to settle these lands
and, rightly, are the truest Australians;
you see it in their blood and hands,
and their ancient knowledge of this land
since before the coming of the white man.
They are the Tjukurpa-Anangu, who
have lived here in the land of Uluru
so long that the land is their religion,
their culture from generation to generation,
wrapped in mysteries we cannot know
from the dreamtime forty thousand years ago.
Their spirits are connected to the land,
trees, animals, plants, even the sand;
and from these they believe they descended.
Nothing we see is taken for granted,
and what we can't see, to them is sacred.
That's why Uluru is a spiritual place
where even the quiet of the desert offers peace.

By the aborigines I have been impressed
with the way they have unlocked the secrets
of the desert of Central Australia.
Today it is recognized as a World Heritage Area
by UNESCO. The natives have built their own
cultural center in Uluru known
as Kata Tjuta National Park,
where they proudly display their native art,
their culture and their use of the land,
and tell their story better than anyone can.

Sidney (2007)

We toured Sidney, cruised her harbor, too,
saw the opera house, took in the view
of the Harbor Bridge, where people dare
climb atop her arch and show no fear.
We visited her parks and galleries in daylight,
and strolled by her harbor cafes at night,
ate in her restaurants, saw all her delights;
but what affected me most, of all the sights,
was the other side of town with less affluence,
which the second class of Sidney call their residence;
and in an old welfare-rented gymnasium
that served as a theatre, where the young
underprivileged put on a show one night,
I saw a black-conscious play about civil rights
with symbols and slogans I've seen before,
and I thought, "This is Harlem in nineteen-sixty-four."
I travelled all around the world to find
some of the same things I had left behind.
I guess the world is no different wherever you go,
and a ghetto anywhere is still a ghetto
where the voiceless, the underclass are scarcely heard,
until expression becomes something with an ugly word.

The Blue Mountains of Australia

A visit to the rising Blue Mountains
brought home to me again and again,
this is a land where nature goes to extremes
bursting with her breathtaking scenes—
her mountains and deserts, her flora and fauna,
her wildlife of all sorts, her colors, her aura.
With the biggest rocks, the strangest creatures,
with primordial beauty, tamed yet untamed features,
it's the only place where kangaroos go scampering,
and wallabies and kookaburras go gallivanting.
In any case, in the Blue Mountains, with its beauty
and spectacular views, I knew there had to be
some kind of legend, some kind of mystery
attached to these formations that stood before me
in the distance, and, sure enough, the aborigines
have a legend, as they do for all mysteries.
As we stood looking out over the Jamison valley
at the rugged wilderness, breathtakingly,
three remarkable vertical rock formations
called the Three Sisters stood and caught our attentions.
According to the aborigines
(who must have told this tale for centuries),
there were three native sisters, who
were named Meenhi, Wimlah, and Gunnedoo,
whose witch doctor father was named Tyawan.
There was a terrible monster in that land,
named Bunyip, who lived in a deep hole.
Unfortunately, Tyawan had no control
of the fact that he had to pass by this hole
every time he left home, and would make sure all
three daughters were left safe behind a rocky wall
on the cliff. One day he waved goodbye
to his daughters and descended the cliff that was so high.
On the top of the cliff, a big centipede suddenly
appeared out of nowhere and frightened Meenhi,
who threw a stone at it. The stone rolled down
the cliff and caused other rocks to roll down.

The wall behind the three sisters split open
and also rolled down the hill, leaving them
on a thin ledge. The angry Bunyip emerged
to see the terrified sisters and surged
toward them. Meanwhile Tyawan, in the valley,
saw the Bunyip close to his daughters, and quickly
the brave Tyawan pointed his magic bone
at the girls and turned them into stone.
The Bunyip then chased Tyawan, who became trapped,
so he changed himself into a Lyre Bird and flapped
his wings and escaped; but unfortunately, he dropped
his magic bone, and after the Bunyip had gone,
he searched, and he could not find his magic bone—
and to this day he is out there, searching and searching.
The Three Sisters, meanwhile, stand silently watching
their father from their ledge, hoping he'll find the bone,
turn them back to aborigines girls and take them home.

As you look at the Three Sisters if you listen you can hear
Tyawan—the Lyre Bird—calling out in the valley clear
to his three daughters, whose frozen stares
are hoping that the lost bone would reappear.
I don't know how true this story could be,
but I was fascinated by its beauty and originality.

Queensland, New Zealand

"Haere Mai, welcome to New Zealand,
and the peaceful little town of Queensland!"
My first impression of this valley town
nestled between mountains and lakes,
whose mountains all around are crowned
with snow-capped peaks, rivers trickling down
from melting snows along the highway,
pristine and clear, "a perfect getaway,"
I thought, while all the while admiring
the green hills and herds of sheep grazing
in peace and harmony, without
a single predator prowling about.
Here, winter skiing in the winter time
and bungee jumping and mountain climbing
in the summer time for some is fine;
but I would be happy just reclining,
or taking walks or going cruising
in Milford Sound, just plain sightseeing,
or breathing in this pristine air.
I welcomed our respite here,
although I had a little scare
riding in a cable car there
to get to a certain restaurant
on top of a mountain. It was elegant,
but next time I'll dine right here in town
in a restaurant closer to the ground
instead of trusting cable cars
that may get stuck among the stars.

Rotorua

New Zealand

Given the name, the "Sulphur City,"
for its overactive thermal activity,
its boiling mud pools, gurgling hot springs,
gushing geysers, Rotorua brings
millions of tourists each year to see
the earth spout geysers with ferocity
at regular intervals into the sky,
splitting the air a mile or so high,
and often emitting an unpleasant smell.
It is a sight that is known quite well;
and in the city they have built spas
and hotels that pipe hot steam into baths
where people travel from far to endure
emersions, seeking some kind of cure.

Rotorua is the place where the Maori people live,
who are adapted to volcanoes and are able to survive.
They are warm people and received us with a Powhiri,
and with that welcome made us part of their family.
They performed for us the Haka dance and
the twirling of the poi by sleight of hand,
sang songs, told stories, served us the hangi dinner
cooked in traditional earth ovens. It was a winner.
They are a non-white people of Polynesian descent
who occupied New Zealand before the ascent
of the white Europeans thousands of years ago.
They are an indigenous population similar to
the aborigines of Australia, though the aborigines'
presence goes further back in time than the Maoris.
A picturesque waterfall against a rainforest view,
and a stunning Mount Telawara panorama disarms you!
On hearing that just a decade or two ago
a terrible eruption had occurred here, too,
proves to me, in nature, that where tragedy exists,
sometimes there's a possibility, blessings coexist.

Fiji

Island in the South Pacific

How fitting it was that the last stop should be
in a quiet hideaway on the island of Fiji,
a romantic place full of mystery,
of beauty and serenity.
Lying on the hundred eightieth meridian,
the International Dateline, Fiji land
is the first place on earth that you see each new day,
with one foot in tomorrow and the other in yesterday.
I felt like we were blessed on that island far away,
named "The Island of Gods," where we met Fijians
who are descendants of Africans,
whose ancestors, 'tis said, came from Tanganyika,
somewhere on the east coast of Africa.
They seemed overjoyed upon greeting us,
their distant cousins from the U.S.

We stayed near the shore, looking out to the sea
in private cabins amidst lush greenery,
and gathered in the main house every day
for breakfast, lunch and dinner repast,
and for entertainment too good to last.
After dinner before they let us go,
they put on for us a beautiful show
with songs and dances that were truly grand,
to make us feel welcome in their Fiji land.

In the few short days we stayed, we visited
a native village they proudly exhibited
where their culture and traditions are kept alive,
and they're devoted to seeing that they survive.
All Fijians, as long as they live, belong
to a tribe, and that bond is very strong.

No matter where they go, they are tied together
and when called must return to the tribe for whatever
duties their village requires of them—
it is the tribe that will claim them in the end.

I met the chief's son, who gave up a career
to return to the village and fulfill his role there.
While visiting the village, they asked us all
to join them in their ceremonial hall,
to participate with them in a tribal ritual
while squatting in a circle around the room.
They treated us like another tribe; as soon
as we gathered, they made me chief of my tribe;
but wait, no one told me what was prescribed.
(I came to find out that a chief, while being big,
has to be brave and act like a guinea pig.)

Their chief and his people sat in one semi-circle;
our chief and my group in the other semi-circle,
and in the middle on a low table, a large bowl was placed
in which some kind of creamy white paste
was strained in a cloth in a bowl of water (I think),
and three or four times during the ritual, we had to drink
from a cup dipped in the bowl and passed around;
but the chief—that's why he's chief, I found—
had to drink first, and last, so if the potion was bad,
I thought, "He's the first one to go," that is sad.
We chiefs drank three or four times more than the rest
since cava juice makes chiefs the strongest and best.
Two ladies in my tribe got emotional and wouldn't drink
even though their own chief drank thrice; you'd think
they'd have the courage to follow me,
especially after they saw me drink three
cups of something whose effects to us was unknown;
but I guess cava juice is not for everyone.
Anyway, the rest of us drank it and didn't get a fit,
though I felt a slight exhilaration because of it.

I learned to speak these words in Fiji:
Bula (hello), *tulou* (exuse me),
and also learned to say:
Vinaka (thank you) and *mothey*,
which was said with a sigh,
because it means "goodbye."

Cruising On The River Nile

Cruising on the river Nile,
I felt the pulse of ages
go coursing through my veins,
as if the ghosts of priests and sages,
pharaohs, kings, and queens,
and people of a distant past
were beckoning from the shore,
"O do not pass so quickly by!
Behold these wonders of the ages
greeting you from the desert,
and all the mysteries you might miss,
and stories that they have to tell!"
Even the river has its secrets
flowing, it seems, forever,
since long before the pyramids.

Cruising on the river Nile,
I imagined I was a prince or pharaoh
on a royal craft with oars and sails,
with royal guards and escorts
and royal garbs and fanfare, sailing
near the shores of ancient Meroe;
or I imagined I was a fisherman
on a papyrus boat or a cedar-made
felucca (still in use today);
or I was a busy merchant on
a barge or cargo boat with oars
transporting goods each day to trade.
Whatever may be my profession,
one thing I knew was certain:
I owed it to the river Nile.

O great, abundant river Nile,
I wonder how people had lived
and flourished on these parched lands,
and given the world such great wonders
if not for you, O wondrous Nile,

who nurtured and inspired them,
who fed their livestock and their palms,
who bathed them, satisfied their thirst,
provided water for their farmlands,
for recreation, bathing, boating,
not to mention, transporting goods
and people every day and hour
for countless centuries?

O river wide, O river long,
the longest river on the earth,
formed by two branches merged in one,
one flowing from Burundi,
passing through Lake Uganda,
the other from Lake Tana
in the mountains of Ethiopia,
joining at Khartoum, then flowing north
thousands of miles through Africa,
as if a kind, benevolent God
gave you as a gift to quench the lands
and infuse life from south to north
across the vast Sahara.

O river wide, O river long,
when I think of all that you must know
of history, events of long ago
in these lands where your waters flow,
of civilizations, kingdoms, empires,
that rose and fell, some washed away
or lying beneath your depths,
I envy you such knowledge vast—
which no misguided texts today
or skillful omissions can distort.

O mother Nile, O mother Nile,
when I think of all that you must know
of the struggles, dramas of humankind
who once had lived along your shores,

who might have sat at the end of day
and thought about their past and future,
and thanked their god(s) for what they had,
lived out their lives the best they could,
and passed on into eternity,
I wonder how many generations
have come and gone? What was their fate?
How many remained? How many migrated
or were removed as chattel slaves
to feed the darker side of man?

O river Nile whose sister rivers
throughout the continent, like you,
have seen so much since ages past!
It's just as well your lips are sealed,
for in the hall of eternal justice
you might bear witness against mankind
who, great as they have been, were cruel
to have practiced inhumanity,
to have conquered, killed, subjugated
fellow humans. I'm sure you've seen
the sins, wars, cruelties of the past
that swept this African continent,
evils such as the Maafa,
the slaughter and human degradation
committed by conquerors, rapists who stole
for centuries the lifeblood, gold,
and natural resources of Africa.

O let me not, O river Nile,
let me not conjure up bitter things
my soul finds appalling, too hard to bear.
O speak, my lips, to better angels,
to art and culture, the greatness of man
that has withstood the test of time.
O speak, my lips, to creativity
and the genius and spirit of Africa.

Let me go back to ancient times,
indeed thousands of years ago,
here in this valley nurtured by you,
to the great kingdoms like Nubia,
perhaps the oldest known civilization,
a once mighty kingdom, land of wealth,
of gold, ivory, copper, ebony, bronze,
with traders, craftsmen, builders of pyramids,
great temples and tombs, with great kings and queens.
Such ancient times might well have been
The Golden Age of the Nile valley.

O take me back, O river Nile,
to the cradle of civilization,
to tranquil sights and tranquil scenes
of farmers cultivating fields,
of people engaged in recreation,
bathing or fishing and trading their goods,
or joining in festive and gala events
when even royalty lent their presence
and pomp on royal boats on the river.

O river Nile, O river Nile,
flowing through the desert of Africa,
if I could go back into time,
and I could trace my DNA,
it might be possible I would find
some ancient relative of mine
had once lived here along the Nile.
Who knows, perhaps you do, O Nile,
for I believe, as many have said,
mankind got its first start here.

O rivers! I have so much respect
for rivers, especially those that are
ageless and vast like the river Nile.

V.   REFLECTIONS

Little Girl, Little Girl

(Dedicated to my niece Sonia when she
was only a little 4-yr old. Today she is
in her 70's, has a successful marriage,
a beautiful family and a happy life.)

Little girl, little girl,
with your dimples and your curls,
with your childish innocence
(Fragile armor of defense!),
how eager you are to grasp
things grownups ignore at last,
but a child will never pass!

Little girl, little girl,
with your dimples and your curls,
with your two bright eyes afire
like the stars that I admire,
and your two frail little hands
touching everything that stands,
you're a joy that's what you are,
more than any shining star!

Little girl, little girl,
with your dimples and your curls,
how you spread such happiness
with your pretty little face
like a prayer in its place!
You pretend you're worldly though
there is so much you don't know;
but until the day you do,
it will never bother you!

Little girl, little girl,
with your dimples and your curls,
you are like a parakeet,
everything your lips repeat!
I have wondered if you knew
whether what you said were true!
You are cheerful all day long,
while grownups worry and frown;
you must think the world is one
big, happy merry-go-round!

Little girl, little girl,
with your dimples and your curls,
with your gift for make believe,
what strange tales sometimes you weave!
How your playthings lie around
you scattered upon the ground,
speaking to you in their tongue!
There are dolls and dishes, cups…
they'll be real when you grow up

Little girl, little girl,
with your dimples and your curls,
when your playful hours are sped
how you lie upon your bed
like an angel, so blessed,
off to fairyland to dream
of sugar, spices, and ice cream
and sights such as you've never seen!

Little girl, little girl,
with your dimples and your curls,
what, I wonder, will become
of you when play days are done
and childhood's a long-hushed song?...
Heaven help you then I pray,
teach you how to find your way!

Truth Seekers

(Mathew 18:3 "Truly I tell you, unless you will
become like little children....")

Here is to childhood days that are no more,
days when the slate was new and sight was pure!
Can you remember the first breath that you took,
your first sense of being, your first smile, very first look,
first happy thought, first moment of childhood?
If we could only remember, if only we could!
We spent our lives seeking to find truth
and found the journey brings us back to our youth.
Gaining was losing and we couldn't understand
how that could be 'till time showed us it's hand.
The paradox of life we could not see
while bound to its mystery. So close were we
to truth at birth yet never knowing why,
though we could climb mountains to touch the sky.
We saw perfection, yes, long, long ago
when we knew not the things that we now know,
when we were innocent before being wise
and no corruption or beam was in our eyes!

O childhood days, O days that are no more,
days when the slate was new and sight was pure!
We grew so quickly, curious, eager to learn--
truth seekers we were without a plan.
A lifetime later and what have we learned?
Not very much except where we began
at the end of the journey is where we must return
after being twice a child and once a man.
The poet was right who had seen from within,
who said, "The child is father of the man."
No sooner born, alas, he is clothed in sin,
losing perfection seeking to be wise;
thus, purity that once was in those eyes...
died when we ate the fruit of our demise!

Genesis 2:17 (...but you must not eat from the tree
of the knowledge of good and evil, for when you eat
from it you will surely die.")

Old Truths, Old Faiths, Old Friends

When through the years I strayed away from you,
not so intending but to face the world
seeking my fortune with brash wings unfurled,
and, in my straying, memories overdue
were pushed aside for things not half as true;
when games, when phantoms and pursuits absurd
contrived only to make my vision blurred
and I groped in a place I hardly knew,
deceiving self, giving false values to
misshaped things and hollow victories,
some wondrous thing, perhaps a childhood song
a stranger sings that echoes through and through,
bursts all the floodgates of my memories
and brings me back to where I started from.

I Never Walk Alone

I never walk alone while I share human sorrow
or joy that leaves its mark! Each contact touches me.
Something is given, something gained with each encounter.
I join in human gladness not by choice alone,
in spite of it -- how can I walk alone?
I share a victory with each human heart that sings
and turn from gloom with every human smile.
Each kindness has a way to move me
though someone else receives it, yet I feel
the warmth as if I were receiving it,
or were the giver with a heart of gold!
This life is mixed with grief as well as gladness,
like vintage that is bittersweet -- none shall escape
who shares the human circumstance! Today we live;
each day we die a little when our fellowman
falls by the wayside, victim of the yoke
that binds us all, for no one dies alone!
I never walk alone, a crowd's beside me,
voices touching mine, cries in the wilderness
echoing mine, a need that is my need,
a hope that is my hope multiplied
all around me, keeping me company!
And so, no matter where I am, I shall go forth,
my hand in hand with all brothers and sisters
beneath the skin...to meet with destiny.

A Life Never Lived

A hand never shaken…
A voice never heard…
A choice never taken…
A world undiscovered…

A joy un-partaken…
A song never uttered…
A love unawaken…
A door barred and shuttered…

A mind never nourished…
A soul never grieved…
A heart never cherished…
A life never lived.

A Frightened Little Bird

One day a frightened little bird
into a room had made its way.
By what mistake it had entered
has puzzled me up to this day!

The door was locked 'till I came in,
the windows shut and all around
no opening large enough for him
to force his entrance could be found!

Fiercely against a wire screen
high on a wall it threw its weight
repeatedly as I, unseen,
resolved to tip the scales of fate.

How long it had struggled in vain
to gain its freedom once again,
I knew not when exhaustion claimed
its efforts, and it fell in pain.

The truth is, it could struggle no more
and so resigned to what lay in store
as its helpless form fell to the floor,
an easy target for any predator.

And, yet, in that bird's eyes it saw
no predator in me, who, tenderly
reached down, moved by some other law,
trying to save it. Quietly,

kneeling I held the little bird
with all the gentleness I could
while not a nerve within it stirred
and I before a window stood.

He looked at me; I looked at him
and felt the warmth within its breast;
he seemed to trust me as within
I knew this was a moment blessed!

And opening wide a window then
I let a gush of air rush in,
which filled the bird with hope again
and made it long to join its kin.

A grateful look beamed in its eye
and touched me with a gladness, too,
as off it flew into the sky
with all its hopes revived anew!

I watched it 'till its distant flight
had reached the far horizon's arm,
when from my feeble mortal sight
heaven had swallowed up its form.

And, silently, somehow I knew
as I had helped a bird that day,
a hand shall lead my footsteps, too,
when I am lost along the way.

The Little Fly

(Who would imagine that a little fly could teach a 9 yr. old a lesson about
life. This one did.)

Whenever nighttime settled down
a myriad army gathered around
the street lamps that lit up our town.
They came like curious people from
the fields and shrubberies all around
the outskirts of our little town
and sought the burning orbs of light
that seemed to glitter with delight
on having friends to spend the night.
They formed a whirling train around
the glowing streetlamp's searing crown,
all night a mad merry-go-round.
Sometimes they crashed into their sun
as I stood there for hours by
watching them with a boy's keen eye.
And if one stalwart little fly,
wounded, fell from its orbit high,
my joy for it unbounded grew
when it had darted up anew
its dizzying orbit to renew.
So, when life's setbacks on me call,
if I should have a sudden fall,
instead of lying by some wall
and trying not to rise at all,
I think about that little fly
that flashes on my inner eye
and rise again to my orbit high.

I Sat Under a Hardwood Tree

I sat under a hardwood tree
and there, above me, on a limb
a bird perched looking down at me
as if I were some pitiful thing,
misplaced and lonely. Quietly,
I sat there looking up at him,
and he, for some strange reason, knew
I was no threat and began to sing,
which lifted all my sadness, too,
to hear songs so enchanting.
Who could have known how sweet and true
those songs would soothe my soul that day?
I'd like to think that little bird knew,
as off to Heaven he flew away.
O Spirit, like a bird you came
and brought peace to my heart again
(and sang because you knew my name.)

The Richest Man Alive

To smile when at the break of dawn
I see the first glimmer of light
rise up from the horizon
and speed away the gloom of night;

to turn away from toil and tears
and pause beside a little stream
to listen to a songbird's cheers
that bring glad tidings to the scene;

to bathe in nature's soothing showers;
chase after fleeting butterflies;
to wade among a host of flowers
and revel at the wide blue skies;

to look up and to see the trees
towering like giants o'er a plain,
dancing and tossing in the breeze,
laughing and courting with the rain;

to see a crimson sunset sky
just as the light of evening fades;
and view night's starry depths on high
and marvel at the heavens displayed;

to share with family and friends blessings
that fill the heart with joy and love,
I am so thankful for all these things
God made that I shall never tire of.

And though I own no vast domains,
no stellar stocks in the exchange,
no private yachts nor private planes
and struggle with bills and with small change;

although I have no wealth to buy
vast troves and goods men pile up high,
yet, with a humble heart and eye,
I think no man is richer than I.

The Greatest Journey

The journey we must make
has pitfalls, that we know,
yet find it hard to take
the path where we must go.

The first step that we make
is not the hardest part
our souls must undertake
to quench the thirsting heart;

but steps that follow it,
each one adding more weight
to test the soul's true grit
and our committed gait.

Despite ruins on the way,
tomorrow is ours to shape;
today becomes yesterday,
which we cannot remake.

Thousands of days from now,
we'll forget how it all began
when our journey comes to an end,
travelling through this weary land.

The greatest battle one wages
is never on the battlefields,
but in the soul throughout ages
with truth and love as shields,

and with a force within
that somehow will not yield
until the Master's calling—
it's all the strength we need.

And if, broken, one stands
against life's greatest foe,
God's word in heart and hands,
only the flesh must go.

Whereas flesh was once nothing
but cold and lifeless clay,
God made it into something
that was not here to stay,

then breathed His breath and essence
into our human form
as spirit that, without pretense,
back to Him must return.

If I Could Save Up Time

They say that time is money.
Well, if I could save up time
like some people save up money,
I would bank a lot of mine.

Think of all the time I've wasted,
that I've surely thrown away,
imagine if invested
what it would be worth today?

I wouldn't even want the interest;
all I'd want are those lost years
that I whiled away and wasted
on an empty bag of cheers!

Yes, they tell me time is money;
but if I could save up time,
I would give to someone worthy,
who ran short, a little bit of mine;

and I'd live some moments over
with the wisdom of today,
when the wine is so much sweeter
and a little goes a long, long way.

A Requiem for Songs of Youth

When hearts were young and eager,
when joy was first in bloom,
time the relentless weaver
primed slower, then, her loom!

When hearts were young and eager,
causes noble and true,
O how a wishful dreamer
laughed at the morning dew!

Those were the days when the tempest
only in name did unfold;
power of the rose was the mightiest,
life was a pliable whole!

Dreams, they were never disaster;
Love was a virgin crusade;
Time was a toy, not a master;
Truth was a beautiful maid.

But, O, the heart grew older,
wrestled the wind and the rain,
and songs that once were bolder
paled in the distant plain!

Sound a salute to their memory,
Time, you have conquered again;
bury the songs in your valley,
sing them a requiem!

Child Of The World

In vane pursuit and dubious plight
I found myself wandering in the night
with mind not thinking, eyes deceiving,
fool's paradise all I could see,
my sanity on the brink of ceding,
I heard a voice call out to me:

"Child of The World, where have you been?
Where in the wilderness have you been
and how did you come so far from the fold,
way out here in a foreign land,
way out here wretched and empty and cold,
poorer in spirit than he who is damned?

Child of The World, lost, gone astray,
pitiful sibling of man gone astray
deep in the dens of iniquity
where abound shadows you cannot hold,
where there is naught save insanity
and greedy Mammon trying to capture your soul!

What were you seeking? What was your goal?
What was your purpose till now never told?
What did you hope in these dungeons to find?
Did you not know? Did you not surmise
while you were risking it all, even your mind,
you were the victim, you were the prize?"

I could not answer, but I knew full well
I had entered inside the dungeons of hell
with all of its trimmings and trappings for sure,
with its demons trying my soul to lure.
Then, about to lose myself evermore,
suddently I turned and I ran out the door!

I ran, yes, I ran with my soul out the door,
everything else left behind on the floor--
my lust and my greed for the things of this world,
my vanity and pride as I fled that hell hole!
I looked back in anger, still haggard, and hurled:
NOT MY SOUL!! **NO, NEVER, NOT MY IMMORTAL SOUL!!**

A-woe, A-wee

O weep you skies! O wild winds blow!
Instead of snow
Let torrents pour
a-weeping and a-moaning.
How came you to this Jersey shore
on a stormy Saturday morning?
I remember now,
I had lost my mind
and was chasing a rainbow
hoping to find
amidst glitter and glare
a pot of gold down here.

I chased all the way
on the parkway
the rainbow in my mind,
only to find
there's no pot of gold down here,
anywhere,
only slick leprechauns
luring you on,
turning your head
with tricks, illusions,
treats and delusions
to steal your gold instead.

A-woe a-wee, what a bitter day,
this stormy Saturday morning.
I can't tell which is worse, this day
or the way that I am feeling;
but the truth is so revealing
to journey this far
where, indeed, phantoms are
and become a victim is appalling.
Eagerly we come
to be undone
by the sounds of sirens calling.

Even the stormy winds that blow
give every hint of warning
to the wise, "No, no, do not go
where the luckless are all swarming
and the price you'll pay is alarming.
O wise winds, blow, blow, blow, blow, blow,
how is it that you did not know
when the signs were there portending?
But the blind won't see, and the deaf can't hear
while sweet sounds of sirens are calling,
"Come to our lair, come to our lair,"
ever so enthralling.

If you want good advice
let this now suffice,
and it will never fail you:
Build your hopes and dreams
on what's real, tried and true,
works for you, simple as it seems.
In a den built on schemes
there can be no silver lining,
just one rule applies to the victims:
Those who build schemes
based on human beings sinning
are the only ones who end up winning.

A-woe a-wee, a-woe a-wee,
what a bitter Saturday morning

Wishing

I once wished I could climb the tallest tree,
defying gravity.
I wished that I could scale a wall
that was too tall.
I wished that I could ride a bull—
that seemed so cool!
I even wished that I could fly
but had the good sense not to try.
O what a wishful fool I've been,
the biggest one you've ever seen.
If God wanted me to climb trees,
He'd give me sticky feet so I wouldn't fall;
and if He wanted me to fly,
he'd give me wings like a butterfly.

I once wished that I was very tall,
but thought it too cramped if at ten feet tall
I had to fit into a space too small.
Once, I even wished to be a clown
with a masquerade and a funny frown;
but, sooner than later, life taught me
not to count on wishes too much, you see,
wishing won't help me get out of a jam
if I don't even trust who and what I am.
There's a reason God made us the way we are
and gave us enough to be thankful for
instead of wishing for this or that
and letting our whole life go to pot.

I guess if we trusted in God's design
we'd be thankful for every detail we find
just the way He made it, His purpose divine,
and we'd be happy he even had us in mind.
Nevertheless, I guess it's a human thing,
this weakness that is not too unforgiving,
that sometimes we still find ourselves wishing.

Some Things We Should Not Pray For

I heard my father say
before he went away,
"Be careful how you pray
and what it is you pray for!
It might surprise you one day
in a mysterious way!"

I wished I had been wiser
and listened to my father;
but I was only ten
and prayed that I was thirty.
But when I got to thirty
I still didn't comprehend.

I prayed and prayed again
and wished that I was fifty,
but when I got to fifty
I wasn't happy then.
So I prayed that I was sixty,
and do you know at sixty
I wished that I was ten!

The Old Lady

(Panama City, 1948)

I saw an old lady standing by
a show case on Central Avenue
gazing with such a pensive eye
at something that possessed her view.
Soon it became to me quite clear
her head was not covered at all
so you could glimpse her snow-white hair!
About her neck a faded shawl
hung down to keep the fresh air out.
The dress she wore (Age could not spare!)
had been a favorite once, no doubt,
when other eyes had feasted there
and other hearts had been devout!
The old lady stood all alone
for quite some time there looking in—
perhaps she dreamed that she could own
what was beyond her purchasing!
A better sense appealed to me
and told me that could never be!
Why would a tired old lady
desire gloves and jewelry
and white-laced wedding gowns? No, no,
it would not do for her to go
plodding along with trembling feet
in such attire down the street!
But I imagined more than that
and saw a gray-haired, old lady
with gentle features looking back,
where the bright flame of youth once shone,
at all her priceless treasures gone!

The Old Man with a Cane

(Atlantic City boardwalk 2000)

An old man with a cane walked in
the sand near by the sea,
stopping awhile to watch the waves
while looking out to sea.
Gripped by the sea, the sea alone,
there on the sandy shore he stood
his eyes fixed on a sight unknown
while gentle tide waves ebbed and flowed.
I wondered what was in the sea
that could command so steadfastly
his transfixed gaze, what mystery
or secret his eyes alone could see
across those waters far from shore?
His world soon gripped me more and more.

Meanwhile two children, dolls in hands,
sat on a bench along the boardwalk
accompanied by two guardians
who casually engaged in talk
about the latest fads and fancies.
Two lovers stood close by a rail,
hugging and sharing amorous glances.
Three taxi drivers sat nearby
their three-wheeled, two-seat taxies.
Under a mild and sunny sky
people walked by in twos and threes
in slacks, light wear, and dungarees.

The old man with a cane slowly
returned from walking in the sand
and looking out, far out to sea.
He passed the little children and
their two guardians quietly,
walked by the taxi drivers and
two lovers holding hand in hand.
He joined the people going by,
not trying to keep up, just content to be
plodding along in no hurry.

I wondered then who he might be!
Some sailor once, perhaps, and he
might have sailed on the open seas.
Perhaps some faraway places
called to him in his memories
as he looked out toward the sea.

Then I recalled a story of an old sailor
who had given up the seafaring life,
who had once loved a maiden like no other,
but the sea kept her from being his wife.

He would leave her, poor maid, on a far off shore
and go off to the sea young and carefree
while she kept a lamp burning bright and pure
in her heart for him waiting faithfully.

"I love you," said he, "someday you'll be my wife,"
and she answered him, "You're the light of my life!"
Every time was the same, "Someday you'll be my wife;"
and each time she replied, "You're the light of my life!"

But the last time he returned to that faroff shore
he had taken too long, too long to return
to the maiden he loved who could wait no more
when the lamp in her heart ceased forever to burn.

Then the sea was no longer attractive to him
for there was no one to return to, no maid for a wife.
How he longed for that maiden with the lamplight burning
and her sweet voice in his ear, "You're the light of my life!"

It made him so sad that he went to sea no more
and cursed the sea for losing the one he adored.
Since that time when it happened many years ago,
according to the legend, he's been strolling the seashore.

All that's left are regrets and memories
of a world he once knew and a love he had lost;
and the sea and the sand and the boardwalk sceneries
are his window through which he returns to the past.

I watched that old man plodding along just to see
where he would go now in his wearisome pace,
and the crowd showed their deference respectfully
as the past and present crossed each other in that space.

Then, after watching him negotiate a stair,
I saw him slowly exit from the boardwalk
all alone, very sad, and then disappear—
an old man from the past with a cane who walked

in the sand miles and miles beside the sea,
longing for the place where his heart should be
while he was painfully looking out to the sea;
and I do not know why he had such a grip on me.

Something About an Eagle Soaring

Something about an eagle soaring
in the heavens on a windy day
when there's a chill and a voice is calling
from depths that are far away.

Something about an eagle soaring
way, way up in the sky
when the earth below seems to be standing
motionless to the naked eye!

Something about an eagle soaring
high above in awesome splendor
mastering the air and wind, controlling
those powerful forces of Nature!

Something about an eagle soaring
on wings with great symmetry,
the higher it soars, the more amazing
are its beauty and its majesty!

God must love eagles to have given them
the magnificent gift of flight,
and talent to see specs on earth from heaven
with the gift of perfect sight!

O for the wings of an eagle soaring
high over sea and land,
far from the troubles and the moaning
and from the trials of man!

I believe that the spirit is like an eagle
priming its wings quietly day and night,
and one day tired of corruption and evil
will make its final flight.

O Save Our Earth from Dying

I wonder why the heavens roar
when heavy-burdened skies outpour
torrential tears on earth below?
Is it because of some great sorrow?

I wonder why huge tide waves break
upon the shores with fury great,
leaving much ruin in their wake
and lessons that are learned too late?

I wonder why weeping willows weep,
limbs drooping down to touch their feet;
why flowers hide their secret tears
behind their beauty from our cheers?

I wonder why trees in the spring
appear dressed up in garments stunning,
but are laid bare and drear and somber
like pale ghosts in the dead of winter?

I wonder why songbirds still sing
so sweetly though their world is dying?
Could it be that they're the world's last hopes,
the world's last sweet harmonious notes

before earth's time clock soon stops counting
due to greenhouse gases, heat waves mounting,
ice caps, glaciers up north melting,
and pollution stifling the living?

The end of earth it soon shall come,
and it will be plainly written on
the final gravesite: This deadly sin,
'man's greed,' was what did the earth in.

For in God's garden He placed man,
"Tend it and keep it!" was God's command.
God gave man dominion over earth and sky;
but what did man do, the willows cry?

What did man do to waters pristine
where species once thrived that are no more seen?
What did man do to systems untampered?
To forests and woodlands that were untrampled?

Man came, lit the flames, contaminated here,
sent pollutants spreading everywhere
and hazardous wastes above and in the earth
that sooner or later for all species spells death.

And every day since, earth lost a specy dear,
be it plant or animal or insect rare.
What shall we do when all the birds are gone,
all the plants and flowers, never again to set our eyes on?

When will man heed the signs of nature crying,
and stop being the cause of earth's dying?
O let it be that this is not the ending
of what was once a beautiful beginning!

Let us heed the signs! Let us hear the crying!
Please, please, let us stop the earth from dying!
Before it is too late, O listen to the crying:
"Save our planet, O save our earth from dying."

When I Consider

When I consider how small is an ant,
how tall is an oak tree compared to me;
when I consider how strong is a giant,
how weak is a baby compared to me;
when I consider how vast is the rumbling, roaring sea,
when I consider how old this whole wide world must be,
I laugh at all iniquity.

When I consider the sun's great light
shining upon the paths we tread;
when I consider the gift of sight,
the picturesque world that lies outspread;
when I consider the stars glittering on a starry night;
when I consider the moon moving in certain flight,
I laugh at all iniquity.

When I consider the changeless modes
of nature's universal laws;
when I consider their flawless codes,
I ponder on this special clause:
"All things in time will pass away that stand:
a growing tree, a lifeless rock, a learned man,"
and laugh at all iniquity.

When I consider that goodness flows
through them who do the will of God,
I smile at all the secret foes
who tamper with the chastening rod;
when I consider the many ways that hate destroys,
I think about the love and beauty God employs,
and laugh at all iniquity.

For Some, Tomorrow Is Too Late

It is sad when a good friend or a relative passes,
sometimes only then we remember a promise made.
It is sad when the past with the present clashes
and we remember too late a debt unpaid.

It is sad when a good deed stands waiting too long
for appreciation and repayment overdue
when you put it off for the right time to come,
and the kindness in your heart keeps waiting on you.

How casually we let life's precious time come and go!
"I'll do it tomorrow," we say, "a little time can wait."
Then the sun did shine and the cocks did crow,
and tomorrow did come but it came too late!

Every moment in life is a moment lost,
depending on your point of view;
but you'll never know how much it can cost
until it personally takes a bite out of you.

Before They Are Gone Away

Where will we go
when there's nowhere to go
without a reason or rhyme?
How will we say
words we failed to say
before they were lost in time?

What will we do
when nothing we can do
can comfort the heart and mind
when the best and the dearest,
the first and the fairest
have left us here behind?

No earthly treasures,
palaces and pleasures,
no earthly kingdoms
we offer as ransoms
can bring back loved ones
long after they are gone!

So while there is time,
reasons and rhyme
and so many words we can say,
do not neglect
what we will regret
if we let the time slip away,

leaving only a longing
that will be remaining,
a longing and an empty cup in time
never to refill it,
only to remember it
in the hollows of our heart and mind.

So, let not loved ones,
parents, daughters, sons,
spouses, siblings and friends
mark time while you delay.
Tell them today before the day ends,
don't let the time slip away!

Tell them now,
tell them here and now
while time disposes;
it's the easiest thing to say.
Tell them, let them smell the roses
before they are gone away.

150

The Man, the River, the Bridge and the Moon

Near the end of the term a certain English profesor
had a conference with each student before exams.
He hadn't the heart to give a failing grade
to one student though that was his intention
for that student's indifference, nonparticipation
and attitude in class, sometimes he slept.
Surely, thought the teacher, he did not belong!
And now he, the teacher, was going to reward him.
To ease his conscience he will let him fail himself
with an assignment that no dotard could fulfill.
He gave him this assignment (which the student calmly
wrote down not even bothered in the least):
"Take these four words: <u>moon</u>, <u>man</u>, <u>bridge</u>, <u>river</u>
and using iambic pentameter blank verses,
I want you to go home tonight and write a story,
make up any story with these words I've given you!
Feel free to apply your own imagination,
but the story must not be less than four pages
typewritten, or one hundred forty verses,
or one thousand two hundred sixty words!
This paper will determine your final grade!"
Overwhelming as this might seem, nevertheless,
the next day the student handed in the paper
to the teacher, shocked, because he never expected
to see the student again whom he was sure would fail
the assignment for he was not a good student in class
and always seemed distracted and somewhat lost!
Surprised, thus, that the student completed the task,
the teacher took the paper and started to read:

"One moonlit night the figure of a <u>man</u>
stood on a <u>bridge</u>, the center of the bridge,
his hands grasping the rail, his eyes transfixed
upon the choppy waters far below!
What brought him to this place this time of night?
This cold and lonely place when he could be
somewhere else warm and cozy? What circumstance,
coincidental or purposed, brought him,
the bridge, the <u>river</u>, and the silvery <u>moon</u>
together in this fixed moment in time?

It could not be a lover's tryst, indeed,
for such a place seemed treacherous, too exposed,
and he was not there with a lover's mien
or happy expectation, judging from
the sadness in his eyes, and his fixation!
What, then, could be the reason? Let us be
the wind, or the night, and listen to his thoughts:

"For years I've sought and chased in vain
phantoms, symbols, fool's paradise and things
for which men vie, strive, suffer, even die;
I've struggled blindly till I found myself
In a place I do not know, a state of being
too alien to be mine! I could not see,
I could not recognize myself! Who is
this person, I inquired, that looks like me,
that walks like me, and even talks like me,
this person whom I swear I do not know,
who grasps at shadows, beats his brains against
imagined walls, who gropes, who struggles, climbs,
who falls, who hastens to his own demise
not knowing that that alone is his reward
and not some phantom prize? Who is this being,

this self-deluding being who tells himself
that things are ends defined in terms of his
primordial appetites, and, furthermore,
possessing them he lives and is fulfilled
when all he has is emptiness? Who is
this creature flailing, raving, fussing with
himself, causing a big to-do, as if
the universe takes note or cares what suit
he wears, what car he drives, what house is his,
or what he had for breakfast? Who, tell me, is
this creature, this mere fleeting speck, who builds
a citadel for himself and says 'I am
the master, ruler of all that I survey,'
who worships monuments to self and sounds
his own brass bugle, bellows, rattles loud

a little while, a second and then crumbles
and turns to dust that's scattered in the wind
like all his monuments, or else becomes
substance to enrich the earth beneath him?
Who is this hapless creature anyhow?
And now I find myself down this dark road
where I once thought I knew the way, not seeing,
just fantasizing; but the darkness leads
only to darkness, and dreams are tricky when
the dreams come from the root of man's dilemma,
and are but opiates to romanticize
the tragedy and let him think that he
grasps some illusory prize. Who is this <u>man</u>
who on this road of darkness having slaved,
who having fought, scratched, suffered, worked so hard
and still no prize? He dares impugn what he
calls 'fate,' that catchword blamed for everything,
that easy answer, tired excuse, when all
it does is alienate himself from self,
increase the pain and hasten his demise.

Here, face to face, I stand with this dilemma!
I see no way—no way!—I can't go on,
not on this road, this dark, this empty road
that leads nowhere! Nowhere! Is this what life
is all about? Is this all that there is?
Here, then, I'll make my stand! This tired brain
and body cry: No more!—better the cold
and friendly waves than to continue thus!'

And as he set himself to plunge, feet first,
into the murky waters, a gust of wind
blew in his face and the lapping waters cried
out from below, 'No, no, no, do not jump!!
Spare me the agony of watching you
sink low beneath my depths, gasping for breath,
grasping, clutching the life you throw away
too hastily! No, no, wait, do not jump!

I've seen too many before you; but you,
at least, I implore before you jump, for yours
is not a lover's cause, or pauper's cause
or one who's burdened with a crime, you seek
for meaning of your life! Wait, do not jump,
you will not find it here!' He hesitated
for just a moment, looking blankly at
the cold and murky <u>river</u>, doubting his senses.

He looked around but there was no one there,
only the night and silence! It was then
the <u>bridge</u> cried out, it's shifting girders straining
in the tossing wind, 'Ho! Stop! Listen to me,
I've stood here many, many years, built by
a dreamer! Many have crossed o'er me, countless
the throngs of goods and people! I have felt
good serving thus, but I was never built
to be used by you this way! Wait, stranger, wait
before you jump! Think earnestly about

the life you throw away! If he who made me
made something good, think of yourself and who
made you! You will not find the answer here,
nor in the <u>river</u> far below, so I
implore you, do not jump!' The <u>moon</u> peaked out
from behind a cloud, watching sadly to know
her light shone down on such a scene. Often
she has looked at men below destroying themselves,
serving the masters lust, greed, vanity,
and pompous power. No wonder so many
are lost, like this one, aimed at self-destruction!

The stranger looked up to the <u>moon</u> and said:
'It's all so good and well for you, you shine
your light on all below and you have purpose
and meaning!' But the <u>moon</u> answered and said,
'And what about you? What about you? You curse
the darkness where you walk, but you have chosen
darkness! Can't you see, you, too, have light,

a different kind, perhaps, only you don't
even know it! I cannot shine my light
into men's hearts, into their minds, into
the darkest caverns of their souls! My light
is nothing compared to yours! The Light of God,
that is your light, the brightest Light of all!'

Those words touched something deep inside! He held
his head trying hard to quell the turmoil there.
He searched now deep within where truth had been
buried so long ago, and then he realized
the <u>river</u> below was right, and the bridge was right,
and the moon shining above in her wisdom
was right, for he never looked towards the Light
while he was walking all these years in darkness!
Then…turning his head that was bent low in shame…
he looked up suddenly to the sky and said,
'Very well, from now on I shall seek the Light!'

And at that instant o'er the darkness rose
a sweet auroral glow that Heaven exposed,
that seemed like nothing he had seen before!
So moved, he walked away into the dawn,
into a brand new day, a new beginning!
And the <u>river</u> was glad, and the sturdy <u>bridge</u> was glad,
and the <u>moon</u>, beaming above, was very happy!"

The teacher finished reading, profoundly moved
and lost for words! He paused for just a moment
mystified! He looked at the student and said,
"Thank you!" It was all that he could manage to say,
then took his briefcase and quietly walked away!

The Masterpiece

(Genesis 1:27 – So God created man in his own image, in the image of
God created he him…)

In a certain workshop just after daybreak
there stood a sculptor with tools of his trade
measuring the task he was about to undertake:
"the creation of a masterpiece out of jade."
I watched him as he measured the height,
the length and width with consummate care.
He studied from many angles and shades of light
the character of the crystals he saw appear
to his specially gifted perceptive eyes
before attempting that enterprise.

In the beginning he toyed with the massive jade
that could test any sculptor's skill and will,
even one who is at the top of his trade.
But a masterpiece demands a special skill,
and jade more so is of the highest grade
like granite only it is much sterner still.
Nonetheless, in the workshop the masterplan
unfolded and the world stood still,
for the stage was set so that zealous man
could carry out his ambitious plan.

Deftly the first gifted strokes he made
as agile hands the grinding did,
and from the mass of lifeless jade
the work adeptly was fulfilled.
I watched the sculptor as he gauged
the massive, formless, lifeless jade;
I saw him carefully engage
his trustful tools so as to abrade
this stubborn jade to make it submit
to his will and determined grit.

And as time passed the sparks did fly,
mind over matter, intensity high,
tirelessly the sculptor dipped
his piercing tool into the hip
and thigh along the statue's side.
As more new scraps were ground away
the sculptor murmured, showing pride,
"Just wait till the appointed day
when men shall view you… they shall raise
my name to new heights with their praise!"

And with these words the masterplan
proceeded well year after year
evolving in the work at hand.
O sculptor with the utmost care
and years of practice ply your stroke!
"Ambition I can comprehend,
but what magic will you invoke
to separate you from God and men?"
He heard me not, and so went on
humming and grinding from dusk till dawn!

The progress of this work of art
was very slow, you must admit,
but you could tell it from the start
that great art does not speed permit
as sculpture and sculptor both took shape;
meanwhile piles of green scraps escaped
and I, in awe, could only gape
at the sculptor while he smoothly scraped
another layer of jaded strips
along the statue's graceful hips.

Slowly the masterpiece evolved
under the workroom's glimmering light,
and any doubt was soon dissolved
in an all-inspiring sight!

The lady's hair stretched long and free
about her neck and shoulders bare;
her face beamed exquisitely
before the dangling, curling hair!
A smooth and radiant smile she gave
that turned beholder into slave.

Within her face the green eyes glowed
and cast a magic spell about.
Such art before has never flowed
from sculptor, I began to doubt;
but there the nymph-like form remained
a perfect shape, a lovely thing!
"How can mere jade," I then complained,
"have any power to rule anything?"
Still, I was spellbound by the stare
of the jaded statue standing there.

I strained to see each measured stroke
and each new marvel thus provoked,
for it appeared this work contained
a touch of genius that is rare.
I saw the sculptor press again
his grinding tool, working with care:
down both the arms and slender hips
grinding and polishing as the strips
and sparks they flew along the floor,
and, thus, the work grew more and more!

Then one night I watched intensely
because the work had reached its end
and I was eager to see a happy
face I was sure I would commend;
but, no, the face I saw looked ghastly!

And, O, the voice I heard was grave:
"I've failed! I've failed! A curse on me
and all the years of toil I gave!
In spite of all my practiced skill,
I lack the gifted power still!"

The green-eyed statue carved in jade,
the lifeless lady that he made
just stood there in the lamplight's glow
with shining, cold, rigid green brow!
The sculptor held a hammer in
his hand, madness over powered him,
and shattered o'er the dusty floor
the jaded statue forevermore...
then wept while all the pieces there
lay glittering in the lamplight's glare!!

Then something happened very strange--
the anger on his face soon changed!
His weeping eyes they wept no more
and turned their gaze from off the floor,
as if his troubled mind was soothed
by some silent, mysterious truth.
I heard him say, his raging ceased,
"I am…I am…the masterpiece!"
And with bowed head he walked away,
and was not heard from since that day.

The interpretation of the poem, "The
Masterpiece," as explained by the author,
is as follows:

Jade represents human nature, one of the
hardest, most stubborn things to work with,
and to mold it would take the sculptor (man's
spirit) more than it can deal with in a lifetime
on earth (the workshop); however, under the
watchful eyes of the Master (the Creator), man
dares to try with the tools that he has (free will,
conscience and ambition) to create perfection
(his version of it). But the perfection God seeks,
unlike man's, is not in the shaping of lifeless clay
into lifeless clay, lifeless stone into lifeless stone,
or inanimate form into inanimate form…a statue…
for all that that is, it is only man's ego and vanity.
The act of destroying it, however, symbolizes the
stripping away of the barrier to the perfection in
man that God seeks. In that act alone, and only then,
the true meaning of The Masterpiece was (revealed):
"a humble and a contrite heart."

Youth Vs Old Age

(In this poem there are three characters, Youth, Old Age, and a wise Sage. The question posed is: Should Old Age be more deserving of joy and celebration than Youth? To the Wise, Youth is only a show of extravagant frivolity, quixotic irrationality, reckless and untested bravura, misguided optimism, and foolhardy arrogance. Old Age, on the other hand, the real champion of life, perseveres and remains with humility to the end of the struggle, unlike Youth who boasts of strength and courage in the early rounds but fades and disappears when the way gets tough and life overwhelming. In the poem, Youth tries to belittle Old Age, but the wise Sage steps in and will have none of it.)

"Drink, drink, Old Age, life's winter years
from vessels that hold toil and tears
and cannot become new again
with all of youth's pleasures and cheers.

Taste, taste, Old Age, harsh winter's brew;
Spring has long gone, nothing you can do
can make old pastures green anew
full blossoming in the sun's bright hues.

Drink, drink, Old Age, life's years declining,
no sleight of hand, no conjuring
can ever undo the handwriting
etched on time's slate unchanging.

Tell me, Old Age, what do you gain
now that joy, frolic, and youth's refrain
are no more champions that you can claim
to raise your banner ever again?"

Thus, mocking Old Age, brash Youth says,
though clueless about what's yet to come,
short-sighted Youth justifying its ways,
deceived before life has begun.

"No," cries the Sage, "it is not that way!
Youth's fun and frolic should never be
life's envy! Youth should be sad, not gay,
and joy should fill the close of day!

Nostalgia for times that are gone
only clouds the mind and makes men long
for brief pleasures they thought they knew
and dreams they once wished could come true.

The saying: Youth is wasted on the young --
untested youth, brash youth unsung,
romantic youth, reckless and gay --
means Youth has yet to earn its way;

means Youth's appeal is a false freedom,
an excess associated with one
too green to know life's limits yet
and the price of each mistake and regret.

The best should be reserved for last!
All joy and bliss that fill the flask
and love should be for a courageous life
that overcomes stress, toil and strife

and not for Youth, not playful Youth
full of toys, dreams and make-beliefs,
not Youth that trifles with harsh truths
before being baptized in life's griefs!

So sing not ere life's battles loom;
rejoice not, laugh not, love not too soon
lest it be feckless folly that is undone
when the real battle of life has begun.

Old Age should be envied instead
for all the victories it has won
while staying the course when Youth had fled
from hardships and pain that came along.

Garlands and roses, songs and cheers
should be reserved for life's last stage
when all the battles, toils and fears
are won not by brash Youth, but by Old Age.

O play the timbrel, sound the clarion
for a valiant life at the journey's end
when the strife is done and the battles won;
and let joy and a great feast begin only then."

The sage thus admonished Youth today
for lacking respect and honor and praise
for Old Age who had paved the way
so Youth could live and have time to play.

"Thank you, wise Sage," Old Age replies,
"Never has it ever been so well stated!
I blame not Youth; they will realize
in time, like me, that Youth is overrated."

The Old Men's Club

There is an old men's club
made up of travelers passing through
who meet sometimes along the way,
be it sunrise, noon, or dusk of day,
and stay awhile revisiting
old themes and tales of yesteryear!
They are travelers each on separate paths
yet moving in the same direction,
who started from a common place
and journeyed far since they began,
travelers who have so much to tell
about events since they last met,
about the past and friends they knew--
some who are gone and some remaining
but growing fewer and fewer still!
They are travelers older and much wiser,
slower from travelling and from wear,
who see in each their own reflections
of triumphs, trials, and despair
that take their toll inevitably;
and from their meetings they each gain
some insights till they meet again,
or their journeys come to an end!

Who really are these old men?
They are boys turned into old men
who could once run without tiring,
race with the wind and shout like thunder
and soar like eagles on the wing
without a hint of growing old!
They are shadows of impetuous youth
who once thought they could wrestle fate
and vanquish fears with phantom powers,
who once thought they were their own masters,
presumptuous youth of untried valor,
who boasted like no pain, no suffering
existed that they couldn't endure!
No mountain that they could not climb,
no challenge that they could not conquer!

O youth, O flippant youth,
you are Nature's trick to fool all men,
to make them dumb before they are wise,
and when they are wise wish they were dumb!
O devious Time that lets us frolic
knowing full well that sooner or later
we shall extinguish like a flame,
no sooner lit, vanquished forever!

Now here we are again once more,
old men arriving at the door
of that distinguished club ordained
that all must join who travel here!
Welcome, old men, welcome old men,
Welcome, until your journeys end!

Who Will be the Last to Cry

If all the flowers die, who will cry?
Who will cry for a summer rose
or a daisy when its life is closed?
If there are no more flowers and leaves,
who will cry for all of these?
And if all the people we once knew
and loved, including me and you,
should die, who will cry?

I cannot bear to think of it
or glean the consequence of it.
If all the flowers that we knew,
all of the girls and boys who
once filled the garden of our youth,
should all be gone the bitter thought
that makes me sigh
Is – Who will be the last to cry?

VI. POEMS
OF
REMEMBERANCES

O Nightingale

(May, 1951, Panama Central Theatre)

When the Lord sent forth his nightingales
into the world it was not to delight
only woodlands, thickets and forest glades,
for one did appear on a stage one night
and the memory of that night stays with me yet!
I remember, O how much my heart wept
filled with so much joy and blessings
that night I heard Marian Anderson sing.
She sang and my heart could not stop weeping.
O nightingale that came down from Heaven!

That Old High School Gang of Mine (2021)

Have you seen that high school gang lately,
that old high school gang of mine?
They were once so young and spritely…
O how life can turn on a dime!

They were bright and bold Adonises
in their prime with stalwart gaits
and could charm the finest lassies
piling many onto their plates.

They lacked not in grit and wisdom
when locked in heated contests;
with sharp wits and with aplomb
they went toe to toe with the best.

They had nicknames you may know—
for in those days nicknames were trendy—
like "Doc", "Lord", "Wicked", "Milt", "Lucho",
"Rancho", "D", " Moe", "Erice", "Dude" and "Sonny".

Given his druthers, "Doc's" yen was medicine;
crossword wiz "Lord" had business acumen;
"Wicked," don't ask me that nickname's origin,
was a great speaker and adroit with the pen;

"Milt" was blessed with gab and gift of pun;
Lucho, an ace pitcher right handed,
was gregarious and liked by everyone;
"D", the encyclopedia, was long-winded;

"Rancho" was a crooner proud of his duds;
"Erice" shied away from too much talking;
nerdy "Moe" always loved using big words;
"Dude" was strange, but you didn't mess with him.

"Sonny" was a radio program zealot,
ended up in broadcasting somewhere;
I, Weldon, they said argued a lot,
(but on that I stand au contraire.)

"Lucho", I remember, had a hearty laugh;
"Wicked" when he laughed too hard would cry;
but "D's" chuckles were like muffled coughs,
"Milt's" grins were frisky when his jokes let fly.

They could shoot so much "bull" and weren't shy
'till I thought they should take a toilet break;
but believe me their powder never ran dry;
and every time they met was like a movie remake.

They were a gang full of fun galore…
O how I'd love to see them once more
to reminisce about the days of yore,
but fate has forever closed that door.

Did any of you see them at any time?
Surely they were here just the other day
bantering, debating in their prime,
full of laughter with so much to say.

Anybody seen that old gang of mine
who were daring, brilliant and young,
the sharpest, smartest gang you could find
not long ago. Now, where have they gone?

Haven't you seen them, haven't you now?
I've been walking the old haunts and streets,
looking everywhere I used to know
in the old days where I thought they would meet,

that old gang; but they seem to have gone
with their humor that I miss, smiles and laughter,
stories, encyclopedic memories, the tone
of their voices like siblings' in banter.

They could spit out more 4-letter words that don't rhyme
and tell jokes to make even monkeys cry;
they could play hard, swear, drink beer and wine,
bleach all night and never come home dry;

they worked hard in school, did their due,
those young lions, future leaders who
grabbed the world by its tail a round or two
and made us proud before they were through.

One was an entrepreneur in his prime;
two were attorneys in later years;
three were school admins in their time,
six were professors with outstanding careers;

one was an advisor to nations who
sought help with tax bases and budgets.
Yes, they faced the world a round or two
against all odds with no regrets.

Have you seen them, maybe by the old schoolground?
By the clubhouse or the ranch where they would meet?
I know it may seem long ago and the town
may have changed, likewise the name of the street;

but have you seen that old gang lately?
Have you seen them, O have you seen them?
Have you seen them in your dreams, maybe,
and heard their young voices speaking again?:

"What's up…" "Don't be stupid…" "Quite possibly…"
"Now don't be a goof…" "Listen here, bro…"
"O Shut up…" "I wouldn't say that exactly…"
"Am I to understand that…" "Well, ah…" "If you say so…"

"Come, come, don't fool…" "Believe me, I wouldn't lie"
Just the way they used to speak in class.
O memories that will not die
though flesh fades away like withered grass!

Years fly too fast, time does not last!
During those moments of good times and fun
we never did sense how quickly the time passed.
What if we could go back and have another run?

I would get to tell Milton some things I forgot,
and I'd ask "D" questions to pick his brain.
Despite our friendship I didn't know Wicked a lot,
but I'd sure like to know how he got that nickname.

Another thing, I would love to tape a session
for hours with them spitting out "bad" words;
believe me, they would beat out the competition
and easily make the Guinness Book of Records.

I always wanted to hear tone deaf Roland sing,
see Dude in drag at a Halloween party,
hear radio buff Joscelyn play the violin
and quiet Eric deliver a soliloquy.

I'd love to see Lucho pitch a no-hitter,
hear Moe recite a speech from Shakespeare,
hear Rancho croon a Billy Eckstine hit number,
and see a school drama with "Doc" playing Kildare.

What I wouldn't give to turn back time
just to see them carousing again in their prime,
just to see again that high school gang of mine…
O how life has turned on a dime!

Have you seen them lately, that gang of mine?
How they could walk and chew gum at the same time,
and sometimes were fiery but you would find
when the road got weary old friends were the best kind.

We were twelve when we started decades ago
and just in a few years we lost nine,
in one year alone "Milt," "D," and Lucho…
O how life can turn on a dime…

leaving three of that gang to carry on,
three of the last fading leaves on a tree,
'til one day when a strong breeze comes along!
(O hang tough till then, we brothers three!)

But memories, like treasures from a gold mine,
shall remain though the years may decline
and shall lift up my spirit just like old wine,
"Au revoir," old high school gang of mine!"

Tell Me A Song To Sing

Rio Abajo, August, 1989, written and delivered on the day my mother,
Philomene Noel Evans, was put to her final rest – May she rest in peace!

What shall a pierced heart sing?
What can two feeble lips say?
Tell me a song to sing,
tell me the words to say
to take away the grief
when a mother's eyes are closed!
O if I could sing what it means,
or if I could speak how it feels,
I would cause the angels to weep
and the grave would relinquish its claim!

If we think that the mind can forsake
what the heart had enshrined long ago,
let that day for anyone come
when one's mother's eyes are closed!—
Then the floodgates are opened wide,
and it matters not how we have grown,
or it matters not where we have been,
there's a bond that can never break,
it's the dearest and first bond of all:
It's a mother's love that knows no bounds,
that reaches deep down in our souls!

O to look on my mother's face
while she lay in her final resting place,
and to think of my life that she gave,
and of all of her love that was mine,
and to think of her gentle hands,
of her self-sacrificing ways,
and of all that she did just for me
that I never can repay—
It is too much, too much for words,
and too great a debt to bear!

But if somehow she can hear my words
from the place where her spirit has gone,
may she hear, then, this simple phrase:
'That her love was not given in vain,
that her toil, tears, and sweat through the years
are the edifice that brightens my days,
and that she shall forever remain
enshrined in my heart and my prayers!

Song Of My Father

(He Bore Scars Seen and Unseen)
1966

I would see him often hold
his hurts deep down inside
as if this life could do no more
than was already done!
He'd sometimes sit reflecting
by a lamp in an old rocking chair
about how the cards were dealt to him,
about things past and things yet to come.
He was tired, his battered body
that was once so full and strong
had been beaten by relentless storms
and tempests, and years of strife.

To look upon my father's features
I knew the pain he felt,
I knew the suffering he endured.
There were wrinkles in his face
and a sadness in his eyes;
there were calluses in his hands;
he bore scars seen and unseen,
and wounds time can't erase.

In despair I watched him there,
no match for this cruel world,
though he knew how to laugh and sing
and love with all his heart;
but what good as shields are these
against inhuman strife,
when the strength of limb and loin
can no more bear the brutal sting!

I looked upon my father,
at the shadow he became
of his former self and stature.
He turned feeble, weak and sad
'till it touched me to my bones,
'till the tears welled up inside!

Yes, I shed tears when I saw him
lying there upon his bed
knowing the drumbeats soon would end,
knowing that he could fight no more
so terrible and so resolute a foe!

Though I shed tears for my father
I rejoiced for him also,
for he played the hand given to him
in the best way that he knew,
and at last for him the strife was over!
Yet if there is any justice,
not in this world but the next,
I am sure he has a blessing
for each scar in life he bore!

Dedicated to my father, Cornelius Richard Evans
who departed this life in the year 1961.

In Memoriam

(Dedicated to all mothers and fathers, but especially those of my
childhood.)

They smile no more!
No more their lively themes shall split the air!
No more their voices ring and laughter swell!
Yet only yesterday their linens hung
on lines to dry when they who smile no more
stood by and watched their little tots rolling
and frolicking in the grass; and as they stood
friends stopped who, passing by, had lighter mail
to share! They seemed eternal then as their
sweet laughter sounded in the summer air!

They sing no more!
No more their lullabies and joyful praise!
No more their gentle chides and sweet reprieves!
No more their kind and loving ways!
No more their proud and happy faces,
as when they saw their offspring off to school,
acting in plays and making speeches!
Yet only yesterday
the world was young and they were gay
and clouds and plagues were far away!

They toil no more!
No more they toil for their dependent ones!
O fallen martyrs! Only yesterday
the hungry mouths were fed, the sick were tended
by their hands and little shirts were sewn
and trousers patched! Just yesterday their hands
had shown with skill the way to use
familiar tools and many eyes had watched
and learned from them then tried to imitate
their skills and practice their examples!

They rise no more!
No more they rise who tucked us into bed
and were the last to sleep but first to rise!
Yet only yesterday they fought adversity
for us and never questioned what it cost.
They healed our wounds, gave us comfort
when we had tripped before life's scars had formed,
when we were still not weaned, mere fledglings,
and gave us joy for our despair, and gave us
hope and faith and courage to face the dark
and life's challenges yet to come, wherein
we learned the meaning why we strive!
And only yesterday
with every fiber in their beings they taught us,
revealed wisdom to us to last forever!

They strive no more!
No more they strive who sat in church and prayed
and sang sweet hymns and showed the way and brought
new Christians to the fold, walked down the aisles
and after service stopped awhile to share
with friends and neighbors, life full upon their faces!
Just yesterday
they made the home at Christmas gay,
they polished furniture, shellacked floors,
hanged pictures on the walls, they painted stoves,
sewed blinds, they hung new curtains, baked spiced cakes
and told us all what jobs to do; they bought us gifts
and made it glorious gathering round the tree!
And when they said, over the dinner table,
"We thank Thee, Lord," just by their being there
their presence added to the bounties spread!
Just yesterday!

O dreaded Death!
O soulless Death! O Death that hath no pity!
Gloat not, gloat not as if in victory,
the victory you claim is hollow… hollow!!
For roots go deep that bind a tree
that bears the fruits that bring forth seeds!...
O memory of them who smile no more!...
Death touched their flesh but not their dreams,
no, not their dreams, their prayers, their hopes!
Is not a tree embodied in its seeds
that grow and blossom in the sun?
Then Death sing not a victory song
for they're not vanquished whom you touched,
their spirits dwell now in Heaven's kingdom!
All you have gained is ashes, vapor, dust!
But they, they gained a victory twice fold:

their spirits dwell now in God's Heavenly realm,
while here on earth among the living still
they live!...they live!...
they share good fellowship with friends and neighbors
through the flesh of their flesh and the blood of their blood
from generation to generation
that carry their genes and traits and talents.
O fickle Death! O simple Death!
So long as seeds from seeds shall live,
here on this earth despite your wretched curse,
then they who smile no more shall never die!

O Tired Heart That Longs for Rest

(To my cousin Arthur Aubert after a Long period of suffering --- 2011)

O tired heart that longs for rest,
that longs for yet that dreads to sleep,
your plight moves not earth pitiless!
Ah, better that you taste a deep
quietus, end all nights and days
and shun this mortal coil that weighs!

O tired heart, your visage dims;
you've lost the fire of better days
when you had championed lofty dreams
and played a part in lively plays!
One part remains, one exit nears
to mark the close of all the years!

O tired heart! O battered will!
Your citadel in ruin lies!
Your troops have vanished o'er the hill!
Your banner fades against the skies!
For you the drumbeats soon shall cease
and crown you with eternal peace.

O tired heart that longs to rest,
how did it all become this way?
How did your vessel full of zest
turn shattered ere the dusk of day,
your leaves all gone, your limbs unsound,
helpless, longsuffering, wheelchair bound?

O tired heart caught in the stream
of life's eternal time machine
that writes our lives across a screen
where features change scene after scene,
your moments were not meant to last,
no sooner born and they are passed!

O tired heart that longs to sleep
but dreads to leave loved ones behind
and treasures which you thought to keep,
nothing remains but shall decline--
even the oak must bend its head
and one day nestle in its bed!

Then tired heart dread not to sleep,
for sleep shall end all mortal pain,
and carry you across the Deep
where heartaches shall not rise again,
where there shall be no mystery
nor mention of mortality!

Dedicated to my cousin Arthur Aubert near the end
of his long suffering.

Fellow Traveler

(Dedicated to my good friend Alvin Roy Williams)

O friend, the years you faced life's common foe
your silent fears and mine were much the same.
We struggled in life's crucible, our bane
was being born poor; yet, our bond will show
somehow we helped each other's creed to grow!
We were each other's mirror whence we gained
insights about faith, life, suffering, pain,
and drew from it courage and hope also.

We dreaded death and spoke not of it often;
and pushed it like a bad dream far away!
Alas, the truth is, it was always near!
And when you lay there quiet in your coffin,
I saw a traveler who had passed this way,
and that he did has made a difference here.

Elegy For Alvinroy

(Written For my good friend Alvin Roy Williams)

O mighty rivers from your depths outpour
your bitter strains, and though oceans of tears
will not bring back his light that is no more,
weep, weep for Alvinroy! O heavenly spheres,
lend, too, your silent reverence to our grief...
give solemn pause for Alvinroy is dead!
His life seemed incomplete, his years too brief!
So many dreams locked in his brilliant head
might still have flourished given future years!
And you, Swift Time, where were you when veiled Fate
issued the call to Ill Health and her compeers
to plague his life as written on her slate?
Too eager then to match your wings with Death
whose only thought is sating his palate,
you, too, condemned poor Alvinroy at length!

O wretched Sorrow, shed your bitter tears!
O Melancholy drear, you, too, now weep!
Go forth and summon all your likely peers,
not to awaken, as from nightly sleep,
dear Alvinroy for he's already gone
where all men soon or late one day must go
when each one's destined hour at last has come;
but summon them that they shall mourn him who
had made the angels proud before he died!
Though trampled and though mocked in his last days
by pressing Death, he went unterrified
as if certain that when the final haze
like clouds had cleared, all would be rectified,
for soulless Death with all his fearful ways
cannot beyond the grave's portals abide!

Come now, you mourners, come, by Sorrow led,
and sing 'midst tears his praise! Who would not choose
to lend a flow of kind words o'er his bed
bidding peace his eternal sleep profuse?
I sing for Alvinroy! How we did drink
youth's nourishment out of the same fountain,
debated often 'till we could not think,
only to find our arguments the same
though our semantics, only, seemed to differ!

How we had sat and played through many a game
of chess and delved through notes and books together
late in the night, both seeking to find truth,
unmindful of the time or state of weather,
but always happy when we found the root
of some great problem through trial and error!

How many times after a stressful day
we rushed from work to night classes together
neglecting nourishment, a price to pay,
denying the flesh to advance the mind, O scholar,
so often there was pain and stress that gripped you
as from a little packet that you carried
I saw you swallow small white tablets, too,
and seem to find relief, still I was worried
for often I would see the pain grip you.
"Alvinroy, you eat too many sweets," I said.
You knew then I knew not your suffering,
"It's eating me up from inside," you said,
"my friend, it's not candy it's aspirin."
'It' was your undoing later, and, as you played
chess, 'it' became your doom and worst chagrin!

For when the pain could be withstood no more
and doctors said, alas, there was no cure --
too late…too late…the beast had breached the door
and viciously devoured his inner core!
Poor Alvinroy, my bosom pal, lay helpless,
strength gone, no armor left with which to fight,
he who often dispatched some of the best
chess rivals he had faced on many a night,
looked up at me, "This fight I cannot win,"
he said, as if I had expected that he could.
"O Alvinroy," of course, I said to him,
"Fight, fight still with your dying flesh and blood!
Remember hard fought battles that you won!
Though this is not like pieces made of wood,
send Death a message: You are still a champion!

If Death were mortal as both you and I
and this was a last round game of chess,
then on this battlefield Death, too, could die
once there was time and with your great finesse,
O Alvinroy, you could still pull through this one
as on occasions through the years you've done.
Alas, Death is not mortal and your time has come!
What chance had you with flesh and blood alone
against this monster, phantom who does not die,
who has no spirit, no soul, no heart to bleed!
O to be mortal in this world, to die
trying to live up to a higher creed,
flesh by its very nature but so high
can rise above itself. O Death, succeed!
Take now your prize, quench now your greed!"

O Alvinroy for whom sad mourners cry!
Now no more you shall play the royal game
you loved, which used to please Caissa's eye,
for you are gone and shall not come again.
How orphaned dreams lean now over his coffin
weeping sadly because their precious home
is gone and shall not rise again in him!
How Hope now staggers with a woeful moan
to think she nurtured him so tenderly,
and, after all the loving care she gave,
after the endless vigil, finally,
surrendered him by force up to the grave!
It is too hard for her when she must lose
one of her own she tried her best to save --
O Death, why did you not somewhere else choose?

Courage, his bride of youth, with pale, pale cheeks
now pauses, shaken, o'er her precious swain
who fought his last fight in the closing weeks --
a champion though gripped with inhuman pain!

Knowing full well the great might of his foe,
and knowing, too, the struggle it was lost,
brave Alvinroy clasped Death as he laid low
and gave himself up to the Holy Ghost!
All this Courage had witnessed by his bed,
and in her heart she knew she had no power
to save him once the Reaper's viper head
had made its wound and marked the final hour.
O Courage, weep for him who now is gone!
That such a promise, such a precious flower
shall no more flourish in the radiant sun!

"O Death, most merciless,wherefore you hate man so
that from his birth you haunt him, plan his doom
and bide your time to strike your final blow?
You have no purpose in this world but gloom;
no loved ones, friends, no kin you can call dear,
what's life to you? Before I make my peace,
why did you not select a different year
for Alvinroy? Even one more year at least
would give such joy to all his saddened peers
to hear his voice upon this earth again,
to hear his laughter sweet upon their ears,
to see his cheeks flush when joy there on reigned,
and see him set upon some problem's core
with simple logic and hear him explain --
just once more with his wisdom! O just once more!"

Death coldly answered: "It was written so!
The finished work is done; it's signed and sealed.
Despite your tears of vain Regret and Sorrow,
what has been is, and cannot be repealed!!"
Alas!... dear mourners, Past Joys, and Passions cold,
and Winged Desires of another day,
Splendors, Past Deeds, Achievements, Triumphs Old,
sobbing in your sadness and your dismay!
Come, pageantry of old friends, all heart-broken,
in slow procession pass his funeral bier!...

...come all, until the last farewells are spoken
under an open sky, then lower him there
and cover him with earth and flowers gay!
Alas!...just one carved stone shall point to where
the clay that once was flesh returns to clay!

O Alvinroy now laid to eternal sleep,
O friend whose spirit now has home returned,
we who remain, our rendezvous to keep,
still strain to comprehend what you have learned,
for now your spirit walks upon the shore
of that bless'd kingdom filled with boundless love.
Why do we weep for him, O weep no more!
His soul is met by angels far above
who see in him their own and who are pleased.
He moves in their society forever
without fearing that joy now shall be ceased.
If tears are shed, shed them for us who linger,
who wrestle with the tides of pain and strife,
who struggle but one day who must surrender
and leave behind the illusions of this life!

To My Chess-Loving Pals of Yesteryear

Years ago in La Boca, my old neighborhood,
when delivering a personal note for a friend,
I saw two grown men at a board pushing wood
shaped like horses, kings, queens and little men.
Instead of going about my business I stood
watching them while listening to their prattle.
I was so enthused by the spirit they displayed
like the fire that drives men into real battle.
As the pieces came off the board I was afraid
things would soon break out into a real bad scuffle
by the fierce language these two addressed each other:
"Fishcake, patza, when I'm finished with you
no one will recognize yuh, not even yuh mother."
And the other replied, "Yes, well let me tell you,
Chicken brain, what they call you, what is your name?
CHECK…bet you didn't see that coming 'Goofus' Tait...
CHECK…where you say you learn to play this game?
You can run but you cannot hide, CHECK and MATE!!!"

I could not understand since this was the very first time
in my life I had ever seen two men playing chess.
As a teen I knew chess was a game of the mind
and not violent as these grown men seemed to express.
The scene was the men' s quarters, La Boca Canal Zone,
and Alvin Williams was one of them who lived there --
In those days he was the best chess player known;
and in bridge, checkers and whist he had no peer,
from that day he was my mentor and best friend.

I'd forgotten my errand now lying on the shelf,
all I thought of was 'I must learn to play this game;'
I was introduced then to the master himself
and I wouldn't leave 'til he said he'd teach me the game.
That's when I found out that his brother Alonzo
who lived there in the same bachelor quarters with him
was the one I really came there to give the note to.
What a strange coincidence, can you imagine!

From that day I learned much from my mentor;
I practiced, read books, studied famous chess games.
Soon I could beat all the old timers! Though gentler
than they were, I never bad talked them to shame
and still enjoyed watching them play each other.
When I played Alvin he had the upper hand
but he knew one day his protégé would surpass him.
We played each other countless games in those days and
though he won most of them, a few times I would win.
Testing each one's strength, taking each one's measure,
the master always pulled a rabbit trick
and I handed it to him resigning with pleasure;
but sometimes I beat him, too, and got quite a kick.

Alvin was a chess lover and organizer.
After he married his sweetheart Dorothy,
one Friday he got all his chess pals together
in his home in the suburbs of Panama City
for a sort of chess marathon, it was something!
We were all fanatic chess lovers, believe me,
Holder, Clyde, Herbie, Pee Wee, Ford, me and Alvin,
and most were amateur wood pushers at best.
We came straight from work excited Friday evening.
Arriving at his home, we were chess possessed
and never stopped playing chess 'til Monday morning
when the cocks crowed and we saw it was first light.
We took turns in shifts playing, eating, sleeping,
Friday, Saturday, Sunday, morning til night,
Three nights and two days for poor Dora it was hell
but she was always so gracious you never could tell.

Later we emigrated, Al, Holder, and I,
still in our prime, more or less, all three of us,
to Kings County, Brooklyn, a place called "Bed Sty",
having left Panama during the exodus

in the late nineteen fifties, sixties, seventies.
We were inquiring if anyone there could play
the game of chess and after many inquiries
were directed to the Brooklyn YMCA
on the corner of Gates and Bedford Avenue.

There we met a small group of chess players who
were rusty or had forgotten all they knew
'cause we beat them so badly when we were through
they wondered where we came from, who we were,
and in no time chess became popular at the Y
'til every Friday evening enthusiasts came there
and that was how we got chess started in Bed Sty.

They soon grew into great chess lovers, though,
Matthew, Billy, Bowen, Milton, Joshua, Ali,
Metcalf, Steve, Chris, Jerry, Herminio,
George and David. Led by Al, Holder and me
we formed a club, the Kingsmen of Bed Sty,
started tourneys, played chess in every venue,
in homes, schools, playgrounds, parks, festivities.
We entered teams in the met league and won a few
top prizes in the A, B, C categories.

Perhaps, though, back in those challenging times
what I remember best were the good old summer days
in the sixties. Those were dangerous times,
the sixties, and yet somehow I wasn't amazed
that we formed a special bond, six of us Kingsmen,
and ventured on a barnstorming chess crusade.
There was sharp-witted Matthew, courageous Alvin,
slang-talking Billy who besides chess played
a mean saxophone. Also there was quiet Holder;
but none was like Jerry, one of a kind,
especially since he was our only white brother,
blacker than the rest of us in spirit and mind.

There we were, fearless chess players young and spritely,
Kingsmen barnstorming city to city or bust,
from Brooklyn to D. C., Boston, Montreal, and Philly,
playing any and all who sought to challenge us.
Any local clubs or prisons, Sing Sing and all,
we respected all men, treated all the same,
took on all comers everywhere we made a call
just for the love we had for that royal game.

I played on first board, steady Alvin on second,
astute Matthew on third, quiet Holder fourth,
Slang-talking Billy on fifth and if need for a sixth
Jerry our intrepid captain would step forth.

Jerry, self-made leader, gave us the willies
often causing a tempest in a teapot
with revolutionary ways in the nineteen sixties
till he scared me to death he'd cause a riot,
challenging every cop, every racial slight
like he wished single-handedly to start a war!
We had to calm him, tell him this wasn't his fight,
to save it for chess which is what we came for,
not to start a riot, not to start a race war!
He would cool his temper just for a little while,
at least until the next chess match was over,
and if we won that match you'd see him smile!

Those were the good old days I remember;
Chess was our outlet, kept us up late,
playing in the streets and in the parks in Brooklyn
while civil rights and revolution had to wait!
I think we kept Jerry out of trouble, anyhow,
or he'd be leading each civil rights parade,
and we might have followed him, too, somehow;
but thank heaven we loved chess –- and how we played!

Those summers are gone now just like the gang—
no more Alvin, Matthew, Holder and Billy,
no more Jerry! But, O, the memories still stand—
barnstorming D. C., Boston, Montreal and Philly.
As for the Kingsmen it, too, came to its end;
the club exists no more, all the players are gone,
most are angels now playing in another realm,
or else moved to another city they call home.

But I'll remember them, best of all Alvin,
my old friend and mentor when I was young;
we went back a long ways before Bed Sty, Brooklyn,
to the quarters in the Panama Canal Zone,
the old timers debacle… the weekend chess marathon…
O how grown men had shown their love for that game!
They were blessed with dear wives who went along,
who, to me, were the true patron saints of the game.

I bid adieu now to those chess pals of mine!
It wasn't for fame and fortune that we strove;
it was something more beautiful etched in time:
't was the bond between us for the game we loved.

She Was Like A Flower Sweet And Bright

She was like a flower sweet and bright
with a cheerful heart and a joyful smile;
she was like a flower sweet and bright,
only here for just a little while!

She was born on an island in the sun
and was raised full of pride and a generous love;
she was born where the heart throbbed with nature as one,
and the soul with the sea and the heavens above.

She was blessed with a touch of heavenly grace
and a childish mischief oft' misunderstood;
there was always a kindness in her face
and an eagerness in her to do good.

She left home, left her island in the sun
in the prime of her youth for a land far away,
taking with her the truths of the world she was from
and a faith that would guide her through life come what may.

There was hope in her heart to fulfill her life's plan
in a country that seemed so strange yet so grand!
But one day in that strange and distant land
like a flower she was crushed by a violent hand!

She was like a flower sweet and bright
with a cheerful heart and a joyful smile;
she was like a flower sweet and bright
that bloomed on this earth for a little while.

Dedicated to Mola Alphonse

I Sing For Clara

O sisters of the sacred well
that lies beneath Jove's throne,
begin and let your hymnals swell
and give this poem tone!
I come to bid farewell to one
who now is summoned home!

I sing for Clara Watley-Paige!
We must not let her essence dear
be swept away without fair wage
of some melodious tear!
I sing for Clara, who would not?
O may her deeds be not forgot!

She loved people, both old and young,
and was a tireless doer
for those whose causes are unsung:
the young, the weak, the sick, the poor!
She loved and in return was loved
by all who knew her here and above.

She knew to sing and was an avid reader!
With pen and wit, a gift for words,
she was a natural leader
who aimed only to serve
her fellowmen before going on --
O what a champion!

Compassion, charity, and love,
deep faith in God and family,
these are the things she was made of
that perish not eternally!
Come, sing for Clara, who would not,
that her good deeds are not forgot!

And though the bitter tears may swell,
though heavy burdens may still cling,
a greater wisdom now compels
this kindred heart and mind to sing:
"A life that was a light shall be
a light unto eternity!"

Dedicated to Clara Watley-Paige who departed
on Saturday, May 27, 1989 after a brief illness.

Steady The Drumbeats Roll

(Dedicated to young Mark Gaskin… R.I.P.)

Heavy the bells they toll
sending their echoes far flung!
Steady the drumbeats roll,
steady they roll and long!
Sadly the sounds unfold,
was he too old or too young?

Was he a man or a child?
Bitter the fate that befell
him who walked here a short while
and paid so dearly to tell
what it must cost being a child
and being a man as well!

Somehow the two must part
and yet remain as one;
but to the innocent of heart,
it is so hard to belong,
harder to follow the chart
and to be weak yet be strong!

Ever painful the grate,
too many choices to choose;
often bitter truth comes too late
after the weak are abused--
to cope thus with cruel fate
always to win is to lose!

He was a child at heart
who groped to be a man,
playing the dual part
that not too many can.
God knows the road is hard,
what with a losing hand!

Was he born late or too soon?
Could it have been otherwise?
Some can dance well to the tune;
others may not be so wise
and pay the piper too soon!
Out of step how can they rise?

Was he born late or too soon?
When was the world any different!
It has no time and no room
to be so kind and so patient
with the young who are not in tune,
with the weakest and most innocent.

Somewhere between child and man
some are hopelessly cast,
groping the best way they can,
fighting a battle they've lost!
He was such a child in this land,
now he has paid the highest cost!

Heavy the bells now toll,
sending their echoes far flung!
Steady the drumbeats roll,
steady they roll and long!
Sadly the sounds unfold
for one who died too young.

Sonnet For Wayne Malik Cooper

(Dedicated to Wayne Malik Cooper who died at the early age of 19)

Toll on, you bells, let wide your message spread!
Your dirges, let them ring! O sad the sounds
that sweep the air and in the hearts abound:
'Break! break!' they peal, 'young Wayne Malik is dead!'
Dead ere his prime and so much left unsaid!
So many dreams unborn and songs unsung;
So many deeds that shall remain undone,
and promises that are forever fled!

Yet...should we grieve who see not past the veil
nor understand God's glorious plan ordained
for all who sleep and who await His call?
Man's purpose is so empty and so frail!
We serve God's will and no death is in vain,
for we, to live, must die; to rise, must fall!

Sonnet For Maria

(Dedicated to Maria Woods)

Sweet were the smiles that dwelt upon her face
as radiance dwells on flowers poets praise!
Worthy the heart, worthy the loving ways
that made her life endearing to our race!
Ever her kindness, thoughtfulness, and grace
flourished even during her bleakest days!
She was the best in all of us, one phrase:
"Earth Angel" fits her life lived on this place.

Now we shall find her absence hard to bear,
shall grope to fill the void and ease the pain!
"Why do the good die young?" the mind inquires;
but be consoled, long life's no blessing here,
or else a rose would live and die in vain!
To serve Him well is all that God requires.

O Gentle Warrior

(Dedicated to Fred Wason)
2009

It seems just yesterday we chatted awhile!
Now gone forever the flame that once shone bright,
the calm, gentle demeanor, the cheerful smile
that formed the essence of his spirit and light.
O gentle warrior, your battered will was tested
until the end, as ours, too, shall be
before the flame of life from us is lifted—
It is the price of our mortality.
O fellow traveler who is laid to rest,
whose earthly shell once housed so many gifts,
sleep, sleep in peace, for you have given the best
within your power to give, and shall be missed
as long as memories live, the past is told
and those who knew you remember days of old.

To Roland

(Dedicated to my friend and former classmate,
Roland Watson. Requiescat in Pace.)

He is gone! Our noble friend is gone!
Look not for him, O look no more,
no more upon this earthly shore,
until the last trumpet shall sound
when all who sleep shall sleep no more,
and Death's mystery at last is known.

He is gone! Our friend from earth is gone!
All that he ever was is gone!
The brilliant mind, the intellect,
the subtle wit, the quiet tone.
A thinker, shy, not much a talker,
his true feelings were seldom known.

Life of the party was not his fame;
crowds and fanfare were not his game.
Yet I would choose him for my captain
to head my best debating team;
and I would trust him though he remained
at times unyielding to extreme.

He was a bright scholar, teacher, lawyer,
astute executive, entrepreneur;
there seemed no height he couldn't attain
with so much talent and excellent brief;
but he competed where they rigged the game
in a marketplace that brought much grief

and setbacks that would ruin most,
yet he was still standing despite the cost;
but only one foe he could not defeat
who came like a thief in a horror show
when he had no defense; still, he wouldn't retreat
and so confronted that terrible foe.

His brave, courageous, embattled soul
faced death the way he faced life, whole,
on his terms and his terms alone;
not whimpering, not even with one plea,
unwavering, bidding death take hold,
he passed into eternity!

He is gone! Our noble friend is gone!
Look not for him, O look no more!
Look not upon this earthly shore
until the last trumpet shall sound
and all who sleep shall sleep no more,
and death's mystery at last is known.

Thank You, Professor Bob

(Dedicated to Dr. Robert H. Beecher)
2008

A quiet giant who could walk
with kings and still be humble,
a man of intellect, thoughtful
and kind, a wise and gentle man
such as you seldom find, he was
a brother to his fellow man,
role model, teacher, advisor,
always sensitive to the needs
and thoughts of others. From his lips
harsh words were never spoken.
He had a way of listening calmly,
of speaking in a mellowed tone
that made you feel at ease and know
he was your friend whom you could trust.
He was a master of the art
of gentle persuasion. Never injuring,
never offending, he could win
you over with a smile and drawl.
"Well now, you may be right," he'd say,
or, "Yes, I see your point, but on
the other hand…" and very politely
he'd make you see some subtle fact
you never even thought of
or somehow might have overlooked.
He was sought often by his peers
to speak at social gatherings,
and he became one of the wisest
and best loved of our elders.

His young associates and students
called him "Bob," which he liked,
rather than professor or doctor.
Added to all that has been said,
I cannot speak highly enough
of him who was a friend and mentor.
I knew him since I was twelve;

he was my teacher in grade school,
in junior high, in high school
and in post-secondary as well.
He saw my transformation from
a once truant grade school brat
to a most improved student and scholar,
imparting knowledge, debating issues,
becoming a teacher just like him,
and one of his colleagues and friends.
But I have yet to thank him for
a treasured gift he gave to me
and do so now belatedly.

One day back in the summer of
nineteen hundred eighty-seven,
I received a small brown envelope
addressed to me and stamped three times
as if the sender was making sure
it reached its destination!
Opening the envelope I found
a note and some old photographs,
pictures taken long, long ago,
as many as four decades or so
when a classmate invited a group of us
and our teacher, Bob, to spend our vacation
at the home of her parents,
the Reverend and Mrs. Ephraim Alphonse,
in Bocas del Toro, Panama.
While there, the group of thirteen went
from Bocas Town by sea to an island
in the Caribbean called Cusapin,
an Indian village in a remote,
unspoiled place. Though adventurous,
we took to the wilderness and to
the native village and the sea
with cautious curiosity.

This was the closest to nature
that most of us had ever been,
and we marveled at that unspoiled place
so far from all the comforts and
conveniences that we all knew;
but it made such an impression that
upon returning to Bocas Town,
for days we talked about the trip,

the Indian words that we had learned:
kukemuko (companion), muko (friend)
mo toboto ari (you are wise)
and kobo kobo (good morning)—
also the things we ate and saw,
the scary nights and scary sounds,
the wind in the trees and the night creatures
shrieking, perhaps trying to scare us off
high in the hills of Cusapin!
It was a most thrilling adventure,
and it was also fun to see
how easily Professor Bob
had mingled and made lasting friends
with the natives of Cusapin.

For many, many years since then
nothing could top that island stay.
Tempus fugit, as always,
that was fifty-plus years ago
when I was only nineteen!

I held the envelope, looked at the date,
and couldn't believe it was already
twenty-one years that had gone by
since I received that envelope
with a note and twenty-eight photographs
in black and white that he had taken
as an amateur photographer
in June, nineteen forty-seven.
He had kept them forty years
in a special box of memorabilia!

I looked at the envelope again
and realized the startling fact
that it was just before his death
when he had sent those photographs
knowing how I would treasure them.
It was the kind of thing he would do,
and it was the last time I heard from him.
He must have known that the end was near,
and I like to think it was his way of saying,
"Here's a gift for you, young 'fella',
something to remember me by!"

I noticed his handwriting was quite weak
near the end, as if he strained to finish
the note, as if he had run out of time!
I looked at the photographs again
that for all these years I had forgotten
existed, and, being deeply moved,
I traveled back into space and time
and relived that summer of long ago.
Thank you, Professor Bob!

But Should We Weep!

The fallen leaves lie scattered on the ground;
a gentle rain this sad occasion greets;
the damp grass bears the tread of solemn feet;
hardly a sight, hardly a worldly sound
that does not lend its harmony profound!
This is the hour, the place where friends now meet
who come to bid farewell with bittersweet
mem'ries of one who sleeps; here, gathered 'round,
the sad assemblage joins in hymns and prayers
and hears the scripture read by him who leads
and lends comfort to those who grieve the most...
But should we weep and dwell upon our tears?
Joy comes tomorrow, so the scripture reads,
death has no sting for us after the cross!

Peter Samuel Martin

2021

I speak his name now reverently,
remembering the past.
He was of great humility,
a man of many virtues
and a committed life.
Though he was never married
and had no family,
and yet he was enriched
by all the lives he touched.
He loved and was loved by all,
even children knew his name
and greeted him warmly.
Devoted to his professions:
School teaching and lay preaching,
he did them both supremely
six days of every week,
one day in the house of the Lord,
and five in the public school.
He never swore nor cursed
nor smoked nor ever imbibed;
in fact, he had no vice
that anyone could tell.
Always neat and trim
with his white suit and necktie,
his straw hat on his head,
umbrella in his hand
whether rain or sunshine
when he walked down the street
he was very much admired
and held in high esteem.
He was generous and kind
and gentle when he spoke
to everyone he'd meet.
He'd tip his hat and smile,
"And how are you today?
And how's the family?
Please give them my regards."

And as the sky is blue,
and as day follows night,
he never changed his ways
nor stood he in with sinners,
nor sat he with the scornful,
nor harmed a living soul,
but served God and man always.
I thought of him just now
and saw him clear as day
teaching a class in heaven,
smiling and quoting scripture.

Then I saw him once again
walking on Heaven's HighWay,
his straw hat on his head,
umbrella in his hand,
tipping his hat and smiling
to everyone he'd meet,
"What a lovely, lovely day!"

To Roy

(Dedicated to My Friend Dr. Roy Simon Bryce-Laporte)

Wayfarer, wayfarer, at last your journey is done,
so, too, the challenges and trials in this imperfect land!
You were a husband, a father, a brother, a son,
a friend, a brilliant scholar, a teacher to man.

I call you a wayfarer, for we are all just passing through;
but how glad I am that we shared many thoughts, too,
and we laughed at funny old jokes, quite a few,
and tricks that nature plays when age catches up with you.

I shall remember you not only for
your accomplishments, that by themselves shall stand,
but because you were my friend and I am sure
that when the mystery ends -- where it all began --

you'll be greeted with roses and garlands and kisses,
and joy that you've never before known,
and your soul shall discover at last what bliss is,
O weary traveler on your return home.

Just As You Are

(Dedicated to my sister Inez Wetherborne, whose Favorite hymn was "Just
As I Am Without One Plea" by Charlotte Elliott, 1835.)

So generously she gave her heart, her being,
her worldly possessions, everything she had!
In fact, if you could classify people
into two groups, the givers and the takers,
she would be at the top of the givers list.
As far back as can be remembered
she always had a weakness (or a blessing)
for giving and for forgiving, for believing
and trusting people to a fault, often
trusting so much that she was easily
taken advantage of, and never would
she even notice! No matter how often
this would occur, her nature stayed the same.
She'd never see or even try to see
the faults in others, as if hoping perhaps
that if she kept on giving and kept trusting,
in the end people would change their ways—
their conscience would somehow cause them to change!
I know some might consider that foolish,
at best naïve; the fact is, Inez was
the kindest, most unselfish human being
I ever knew — too kind, perhaps too gentle
and far too good in nature for this world!
Goodness like hers too often is abused
by others and too often is exploited.

She never did complain about anything,
about the meanness, cruelty around her,
and least of all, how others treated her.
She never even winced or spoke about
her own suffering and pain. Often she'd be
feeling excruciating pain, yet if
you asked her how she felt she'd always say,
"I'm feeling all right," though you knew she wasn't.

She kept her suffering to herself as if
to her, her whole life was a kind of penance—
or a sacrifice to endure until the end.
Like Job, she'd bear it all, however harsh,

and she would wait patiently for God's judgment,
knowing that when He called He would find her
true to that heavenly nature that He gave her.
This world could take away all her possessions,
all her material goods, all that she owned,
even her flesh and blood and still not take
away her goodness of heart, kindness of soul,
trust in God. The first things they can take;
the latter she shall keep with her in Heaven.
O my dear sister, genuine and true!
O patient, giving child of God, return now
to your Maker! He will give you peace
and your rewards which you richly deserve,
"just as you are, without one single plea!"

O Captain! O Captain!

(Dedicated to Laura La Bon Higgins, former Director of the Manhattan Educational Opportunity Center who returned home in November, 2003.)

O Captain! O Captain!
How pale and still you lie!
No more your valiant spirit
shall guide our ship at sea!
No more your voice shall sound
its clarion call so clear!
No more to set the bar for us,
to cheer us on to newer heights
and goals year after year.
No more to inspire and upbraid us,
to console us and to share our personal griefs.

O Captain! O Captain!
How pale and still you lie!
Too swift, proclaims the heart,
too swift the dark night came
and stole you from our helm!
You've led us well over rough seas
and fought so many battles
with mighty pen, with matchless wit,
with courage and with wisdom—
and never lost a fight—till now!

O Captain! O Captain!
How pale and still you lie!
We've seen you wrestle this last foe
and watched you bend but still not break,
and prayed for our dear captain
that you might win this battle yet
and be yourself once more—
but that was not to be!

O Captain! O Captain!
How pale and still you lie!
How many orphaned dreams and thoughts
and visions that once flourished
are now forever fled
from so brilliant a head!
We might have shared those dreams,
alas, who shall pursue them now!

O Captain! O Captain!
How pale and still you lie!
No more your love for children shall you manifest,
no more to hug and cuddle them in your arms!
We watched you give your heart to them
time after time and never tire as they returned your love!
And to your friends and staff your kindness knew no bounds,
nor your compassion for others facing hardship!
You were so strong—and yet so gentle.
You were so firm—and yet so fair.
You were so great—and yet so humble.
You were so serious—yet light-hearted.
You were the exemplar of a friend,
a fighter, leader, lady, all in one.

O Captain! O Captain!
How pale and still you lie!
When shall there be another
like you to guide our ship!
You knew this ocean like a book:
this city, town, the people in it, great and small!
You knew the who, where, when, what and how
to pave the way and get things done!
And how you loved this Harlem and the people in it!
And how you loved this school, this ship The E.O.C.!

O Captain! O Captain!
How pale and still you lie!
Thanks to the keel you helped to build,
this ship shall still sail on…
but what of you, my Captain, what of you!
I pray, throughout the years to come,
may we never forget you!
O well that we should honor you,
your life was like a light
that shall shine throughout eternity.

For My Dear Sister Who Passed I Sing

(Dedicated to my sister, Fermina Evans-Edghill who departed on April 10,
1999.)

For my dear sister who passed I sing
so that her essence dear
is not swept away without offering
a prayer or melodious tear.
I sing her praises, who would not,
and may she never be forgot!

All the love and joy she gave
and memories sweet Death cannot quell.
So much of her beyond the grave
lives on in us who loved her well.
A heart that shared her love and kindness
cannot forget such blessedness.

We knew her and we never thought
the morning sun could shine without
her presence and the gifts she brought;
but we were too spoiled to know doubt,
and only now we miss what were
the treasures of her sweet nature.

Like a flower she was planted here
to bloom in our sight and God's light.
Her strength was tested, grief her seer;
She bore her pain with gentle might,
kept faith throughout the darkest night,
and looked with pity on pain and slight.

And when all strife and grief were done,
as she passed through death's open door,
for her no more shall weeping come,
no more dying, no more, no more!
Into the garden of love and delight
her spirit now soars where there's no night.

The House on Lafayette Avenue

There was once a time not long ago
when all roads seemed to lead you there
and every week a constant flow
of people came from everywhere.
Some found their way there through the years
seeking light and encouragement
while passing through. Youths on their own
facing a harsh predicament
while studying, struggling far from home
with only a dream, sometimes no clue,
would often find their way there, too,
to the house on Lafayette Avenue,
and were welcomed by someone who
with open arms showed them the way,
helped them through hard times they would meet,
and gave them nurture and a place to stay
until they got back on their feet.

How many lives throughout the years
did that house on Lafayette Avenue touch?
How many young scholars, now with bright careers,
to that cherished abode owe so much?
How many people have broken bread there
and joined in prayers and shared good cheers?
There was something special at that address,
I think the magic was simply this:
that House on Lafayette Avenue was blessed,
and the blessings that dwelled within that home
were the goodness and charity of one Aunt Ness
and her Dear Sam, her quiet champion.

If you had known Anesta and Sam
and spent an evening in their home;
if you had chatted with them awhile
and heard them in their humble tone
speak of their values and their beliefs,
how the mission of helping others alone
brought them such joy and fulfillment;

if you had visited them on any evening,
whether or not there was a special event
like a meeting or just friends socializing,
(notwithstanding a crowd, which was not surprising),
you would know their genuine love and warmth;
you would know their generous hospitality
and why that house on Lafayette Avenue
was a special place, a second home to many;
why it was an anchor, guiding light and beacon to
so many young people who once stayed there
and went on to achieve successful careers;
you'd know why so many friends came from far away
to meet and to share rich memories there;
and you'd know why that avenue is renamed today:
the S. Anesta Samuel Avenue.

Now, both Anesta and Sam are gone;
and there are no more gatherings there today
at two-seventy-six Lafayette Avenue,
Brooklyn, New York, U.S. A. ;
but if you should ever pass that way,
look up at the street sign and the house that is near,
and give a brief pause before you walk away,
and pay a tribute to the couple who once lived there,
and the lives made better because they were here!

A Remarkable Lady

(2013)

Not long ago while undertaking
tidying up my home, discarding
old books I deemed not worth keeping,
a certain lady said to me:
"Give me those books for the poor and needy.
What you call old books I've shipped many
to African school children in need,
who have so very few books to read.
I know an agency that sees to it
that books from kind donors are shipped
to places where they're most needed --
a shame these books should go wasted."

Those words from a remarkable lady
conveyed to me unbounded energy,
which she lacks but having such a strong will,
even pain could not keep her from work she must fulfill.
In addition to charitable work that she does,
despite her schedule that hardly allows
much of anything else, she plans trips each year
and a nucleus of close friends are sure to be there.
On a recent trip to Ghana, 'twas no surprise
she brought with her gifts and school supplies
for a remote village school that we visited.
It wouldn't have been her to go empty-handed.

She is active in many organizations
and is often invited to public functions.
As a mature adult of character and grace,
she carries herself ladylike with taste,
and is distinguished by her smart attire,
always well-groomed as the occasions inspire.
She has been a member, officer, founder
of several non-profit organizations over

the years that contribute to the wellbeing
of the community in many areas, including:
youth scholarships, teen guidance, women's health,
elder care, nursing and art; and her wealth
is the thanks and recognition that have come
from all the good work that she has done.

She is also a defender, advocate, activist
and promoter for striving and struggling artists,
especially in the African-American community,
through one of the organizations that she
is a member and founder of, Heart to Art.
She creates a venue, a forum, for their art
to be seen and to be exposed to many
unaware of this treasure in our society.
She sponsors luncheons honoring them
and exhibits their talents for which they acclaim
her with grateful hearts as a dear patron,
for through her they know their work lives on.

She is a natural leader and though you can tell
that her friends all have leadership skills as well,
being gifted professionals in their own right,
yet I always admire the way they delight
in her friendship, leadership, collegiality and intellect,
and work with her and for her with mutual respect.
She is the one to whom they all defer
and her approval is always sought after.
She never shouts or shows displeasure,
never thinks of herself first, but of others;
and everyone knows, as the sun shall rise,
she's trustworthy, fair-minded, thoughtful and wise.
She'll never disappoint and whenever you realize
that someone had your back, if you didn't know who,
you can bet she was the one looking out for you.

Ever since I can remember, she has worn
the mantle of a kind and thoughtful person
who cares for others, especially the sick, the poor,
the young and the elderly. An unselfish doer,
her whole life is built around the same tenets.
It is in her blood, indelibly in her precepts,
it is in her genes, and in her D.N.A.
She comes from a line, going back a long way,
of women who were givers and people servers,
a line of very active community leaders,
at least three generations who came before her,
who were tireless torchbearers in helping others.
The torch was first given to her grandmother,
who passed it on to the next generation,
her mother and two aunts, who then passed it on
to her, her sister and cousin who have borne
the torch well, continuing in the same tradition.

There are so many causes that she has championed
and lives she has touched throughout the years
that if they were all seen from the stratosphere
as points of light, figuratively,
sourced from her candle of service ever since she
began to serve, I believe a very good part
of the earth would be lit from heart to heart
spreading afar the light that she passes on.
Since good always comes from good every one
of her deeds is therefore truly a blessing
that keeps on spreading and keeps on returning,
like endless ripples in a pool
spreading blessings and the wider the pool,
the more the ripples keep on spreading still.
I can only imagine if somehow we could fill
the world with lives and souls that are dedicated
to lifting up others, and if her example were replicated
a thousand times ten thousand times,
then that, to me, would be divine,
for it is God's love enriching mankind.

Dedicated to Grace Y. Ingleton, a remarkable lady.

When a Great Light Goes Dim

(Dedicated to Grace Y. Ingleton)
2021

When a great light goes dim,
in its final hour declining,
it senses that its brilliancy
is no more what it used to be;
and O 'tis hard when such a light,
that once had been so warm and bright,
loses its brightness and its glow
that we had come so well to know.

When a great light goes dim,
in its final hour declining,
it does not want to let darkness
shut off its love and goodness,
and wants to shine its power still
to fight the dark with all its will,
but, O, 'tis hard when such a light
can no more fight the good fight!

When a great light before our eyes
goes dim, flickers, and then dies,
our first sense is of bitter grief,
of hollowness, of disbelief!
We pause wanting to turn back Time
and capture past moments sublime.
How can there be a better day,
we ask, now that she's gone away?

When a great light before our eyes,
goes dim, flickers, and then dies,
it is so sad to lose that light
if that were all… and then goodnight!
But there are countless candles bright
that were lit by that great, great light
still shining with her love! They cry:
she did not die, she did not die!

When you always live for others, 'tis true,
others will always live for you.
In every heart that had been known
to walk in her light, Grace has a home.
For her to die means we never lived
and darkness over light had thrived.
Therefore, she did not die but shall be
a light shining 'till eternity.

VII. COME WALK WITH ME DOWN MEMORY LANE
AND
OTHER POEMS

Come Walk With Me Down Memory Lane

Come walk with me down Memory Lane
and see a lost town once again
where crotons and hibiscus flourished
and shy mimosas used to blush
and close their eyes to the slightest touch,
where vegetation was so lush
your clothes would stick on a macca bush.

Come walk with me down memory lane
where the grass grew tall and if it rained
we would not even need an umbrella,
we would take shelter "under a cellar",
and play dominoes 'till the rain blew over;
and then look up at the clear blue sky
and trace a rainbow with the naked eye.

Come walk with me down memory lane
along familiar routes again,
where coconut trees lined the widest street
and mango trees provided a treat
in all varieties that you can eat.
We'll pass by the old breadfruit tree again
and the sour sap, guava and the tamarind.

Come walk with me down Memory Lane
and roast some corn and eat sugar cane,
and roast sweet potatoes and cashews by the fire,
tell funny jokes, sing calypsos we desire
and eat and laugh until we tire,
or our parents called out to let us know
it was time for us children to retire.

O come to a land I used to know
where one of my friends was a buffalo
and another a sling shot I would not let go
while tracking lizards to their lair.
We'll watch humming birds stop in mid-air,
and wait in the bushes for birds to come
and we'll see where swallows make their home.

O come with me, O come with me
and see the sights that used to be,
in a magical town near by the sea
where the view of ships and the sea was profound,
and fresh ocean breezes cooled the tropic sun,
where in the distance the sky came down
and kissed the sea on the horizon.

O come with me to memory town
where boys wore fine shirts and shark skin pants,
and girls wore matching skirts hand sown,
when they dated and went to a festive dance,
sometimes under the lens of watchful eyes;
but youth would always pull a surprise
and break curfew and come home at sunrise.

Come walk with me through the town park
when the sun went down and it got a little dark,
but a full moon light would make it so bright
you could play pitch and catch as in daylight.
If the night was too dark we could still dilly dally
and see by the light of the *pee-nee-wally*
and try to catch a few if we were lucky.

Come walk with me down memory lane
when a *nyap* was in circulation back then,
though it might seem a long, long way,
when a nickel and a *quatti* could last a whole day.
We'll see what it's like when we make a stop
on a Sunday morning by the Chinese shop
and for a quarter buy an awful lot:

We'll buy a cup of rice, some hard biscuits,
a half stick of butter, some brown sugar, too,
a penny's worth of cigarettes,
five cents worth of lettuce and tomato,
and for *pesuna,* get a piece of *rapaduro*.
Good thing there was a Chinese shop
open on days the commissary was not.

Come walk with me, 'twill be a delight
to taste stew chicken and rice, plantain, too,
and *labadee* sauce to whet your appetite,
or swim in some *cowfoot* soup or beef stew,
or smack your lips with codfish and *callaloo*;
and there's a tall glass of sorrel just waiting for you
to wash it down, maybe two glasses will do.

O come with me down Memory Lane
and see the sights, hear sounds again
of laughter coming from the street,
where Mr. Armstrong in a funny clown suit
would dance with a clownish, raggedy beat
to the twists and turns of the *gully root*,
collecting pennies and nickels to boot.

O come with me down Memory Lane;
see the Salvation Army band marching again;
see Ms. Agard with triangle and tambourine
followed by the bass drum and brass section playing,
"Onward Christian soldiers marching on to war
with the cross of Jesus going on before,"
two blocks up San Domingo to the little church door.

Come walk with me down memory lane
and see familiar faces again:
the boys and girls next door, classmates in school,
the bullies, the heroes, the lifetime friends we made,
the grownups, our role models, mostly serious as a rule,
the teachers who taught us well but were underpaid,
our parents whose pride showed when we made a good grade.

Come walk with me down memory lane
where we played stickball when it did not rain,
where we played in the clearings between buildings,
where a tree or a house post was an imaginary base,
where the outfield was as far as a ball could go sailing,
and the home plate was a patch in the ground we traced
or a stone or a marker we happened to place.

Come walk with me at five in the morning
when the grass was wet from dew drops forming
and the morning mist was still prevailing,
and hear the first brave rooster crowing
with other roosters joining in,
while the street lights were still lit up in town
as the morning work crew were leaving home.

Come see the glimmer of the sun rising
while the rest of the town were just awaking,
and children very soon were off and running
when the school bell began its final ringing,
and you knew who would be at the main door waiting
to remind latecomers entering,
there's a price to pay for lateness in the morning.

Come walk with me to memory town
and see the gatherings, games, and rallies
converging on the public ball ground,
when all the Toms, Sams, Freds and Sallies
joined in the fun and festivities,
if only for a day of memories
to share later with friends and families.

Come walk with me to memory town
and catch a glimpse after five near sundown
of carpenters, boat builders, tinsmiths, craftsmen
in their spare time under the cellars building
things like boats, furniture, and stoves made of tin.
Everything they built with gifted hands
and skills brought from their homelands.

Come walk with me down memory way
when workers on their holiday,
on a Saturday morning in the dry season,
played a sport for gentlemen, I reason,
called cricket, in white suits, white shoes and hat.
In any other sport they'd be dirty in that
outfit before they even came to bat.

Come walk with me down memory lane;
We'll pass by the icehouse once again
in the early morning on a Saturday
and see folks buying ice by the pound
to keep their ice boxes cold all day.
As a boy I made tips delivering ice home
in a crocus bag, in a cart or a wagon.

Come go with me down memory lane
And walk by the commissary once again
And stop by the kerosene section where
we'll listen to "Pajac" recite Shakespeare
and poetry with his eloquent flare,
while we buy kerosene and linger there,
reluctant to miss a performance rare.

Come walk with me down memory lane
and walk by the seashore once again,
past the ferry going east when the tide was low;
and toss some flat stones just to see
how many times you can make one go
skipping on the surface of the sea.
Though it's not the record, I once made three!

Come walk with me down memory lane
on the railroad tracks by the sea when the train
was not in sight. We had no fear
and walked to the first pier to go fishing there.
Sometimes we went further past the oil landing pier
for miles till we reached an army fort,
when our adventure seemed to lose its sport!

Come walk with me down memory way
on a Sunday which was the holiest day.
No one cursed or swore on a Sunday,
the worst sinners behaved like saints;
everyone dressed up and went to church;
there were no crimes and no complaints;
it was the most peaceful day on earth.

Come walk with me down memory lane
to a place where being poor was no shame,
where people had pride, character, faith in above,
and gained strength to bear with hardships each day
knowing their families were fed, cared for, and loved
and had a better future by their paving the way.
That they were right, time alone had the last say.

Come walk with me to memory town,
before the winds of change had come,
before fledglings outgrew their nests,
before the sights changed that we knew best
and mornings had a different sound,
when there were no more roosters around
and no more vendors passing through town.

Come walk with me to memory town
before the houses were all torn down
and the coconut, sour sap, mango trees we loved,
and the tamarind, breadfruit trees were not spared
but were all rooted up and destroyed or moved;
and the sidewalks and streets were dug up and cleared,
and everything and everyone we knew disappeared.

Come walk with me down memory lane
when we were young and knew no pain
that grips the soul and clogs the vein,
when for a little while we knew
a place on earth we once called home,
but can no longer return to, ·
except on Memory Lane alone.

Dedicated to a silver town once known
as La Boca, Canal Zone.

Land Where My Father Labored and Died

(Silver workers burial ground, Corozal Cemetery, Panama, C.Z.)
2003

O land where my father labored and died
and where my mother now lies by his side,
both sleeping on a very quiet hillside
where many sons and daughters abide;

O land that once divided two oceans
until bold and relentless excavations
gouged out your stubborn mountainsides,
stirring your wrath that unleashed bitter landslides;

O land where brave Caribbeans once stood
and toiled and sacrificed their precious blood
so that two mighty oceans could meet
and many nations prosper at your feet;

O land of my birth where long, long ago
countless dramas played out and life springs flowed
from so many brave men and women although
the world acknowledged not nor cared to know;

O land that has taken and given in return,
whose gifts to man our forebears more than earned
and paid for drop by drop while being spurned
and cast aside like shoes grown old and worn;

O land, where is justice? Is there none
for them who toiled here and now are gone?
They weren't even welcomed at the feast
after they gave the most and gained the least!

O land, O fair-minded justice (if there is such),
if you know the answer tell me it's not too much
to ask why on this grassy, ill-kept hillside
our fathers' graves are strewn carelessly aside

till even weeds gain more respect and flourish
while covering o'er the graves of those we cherish?
Here on this open, soggy field, it's hard to find
even a name or stone of any kind!

O tell me we owe them more than this!
The silent voices of the dead insist,
"Forget us not here among these weeds
that are degrading to our past lives and deeds.

If we meant anything, if there was worth
in our struggles once upon the earth,
forget us not and cast us not aside
as if we never strived and for nothing we died."

I glance now at this field of fallen men
and women whose kind we'll never see again,
this remnant of the "silvermen" who came
from far across the seas and helped to tame

a jungle, brave its hazardous terrain,
carve out its mountainsides in sun and rain
at the highest cost of blood and human pain,
and I wonder did they sacrifice in vain?

Is this the thanks then that we give to them,
to lie unhallowed, neglected, and condemned
to the ravages of soggy grass and weeds,
forgotten like forgotten debts and deeds?

O land where brave Caribbeans once stood
and toiled and sacrificed their precious blood,
if not for them who paved for us the way
where would we be, where would we be today?

O land, in the name of justice and respect,
however long before it takes effect,
cry out, cry out to all humanity,
"O treat this resting place with dignity!"

The Old Timer

(Washapali, Panama, 1980)

I saw him there looking feeble and cold,
a remnant of what was once called a man,
cuddled 'neath sheets, straining to raise his hand
to greet me as I entered his abode –
a dark and dusty room with pieces old:
a broken chair, stove, table and wash pan.
He could not walk; he could not even stand!
His weary eyes and voice both touched my soul!

Here was a man who was once proud and strong,
whose sweat and blood helped build a great Canal
from which nations have prospered…but not he.
How was he thanked when all his strength was gone?
Not even a paltry pension for it all…
But left to die here in obscurity!

Wayfarer, Wayfarer, Where Is Your Home?

Wayfarer, wayfarer, where is your home?
Where is that place where you belong?
You've looked everywhere and then some,
even in places Father Time has abandoned.

Wayfarer, wayfarer, where is your home?
If you only had a compass to guide you there!
Perhaps it's in the mountains or beyond;
perhaps in the skies up there somewhere

beyond the farthest star. O could that be?
Or else in a vision, or a shadow or a dream,
or a distant paradise in some distant valley
yet to be found in another realm?

Wayfarer, wayfarer, just passing through,
deigning not to stay in this imperfect land,
when you find where you belong they shall welcome you
and the mystery shall end where it all began—

and they'll greet you with roses and garlands and kisses,
and joy that you've never before known;
and your soul shall discover what true bliss is,
O traveler, at last when you've come home.